Between the Lines

jason donovan

jason donovan

Between the Lines

My Story Uncut

HarperCollins*Publishers*

HarperCollins*Publishers*
77–85 Fulham Palace Road,
Hammersmith, London W6 8JB

The HarperCollins website address is: www.harpercollins.co.uk

First published by HarperCollins*Publishers* 2007

1 3 5 7 9 10 8 6 4 2

© Jason Donovan 2007

Jason Donovan asserts the moral right to be
identified as the author of this work

A catalogue record of this book is
available from the British Library

HB ISBN-13 978-0-00-726147-5
HB ISBN-10 0-00-726147-0
PB ISBN-13 978-0-00-726441-4
PB ISBN-10 0-00-726441-0

Printed and bound in Great Britain by
Clays Ltd, St Ives plc

All photographs have been supplied by the author, with the exception of: Alan
Davidson/Rex Features/Edward Hirst/Solo Syndication/John Frost Archive: p13 (top);
The Australian Postal Corporation/The National Philatelic Collection: p5 (bottom left);
Barnaby J. Watson: p20; Dave Bennett/Getty/Solo Syndication: p11 (bottom); Dean
Gaffney: p18 (bottom); Dewynters/Michael Le Poer Trench: p14 (bottom left);
Fremantlemedia Stills: p7 (middle); ITV/Rex Features: p18 (top); John Dee/Rex
Features: p5 (top); John Fairfax Publications Pty Ltd: p1 (top); Jonathan Shteinman:
p11 (middle), p12 (all), p13 (middle); Lawrence Lawry Idols: p24 (top); Leon
Neal/AFP/Getty Images: p21 (top); www.lfi.co.uk: p5 (bottom right), p7 (top left);
Mirrorpix: p9 (middle); Nils Jorgensen/Rex Features: p6 (top), p14 (top); Pal
Productions Ltd: p6 (bottom); Peter McConchie: p10, p16; Simon Fowler/Emap/Vinmag
Archive Ltd: p7 (top right); Simon Fowler: p8, p17; Sony BMG Music Entertainment
(UK) Ltd: p6 (middle); *The Sun* (05/05/1989)/N.I./Syndication Ltd/John Frost Archive:
p9 (top); *The Sun* (17/08/1989)/N.I./Syndication Ltd/John Frost Archive: page 9
(bottom); www.swd.co.uk/Hugo Glendinning/The Rocky Horror Company: p10 (inset).

While every effort has been made to trace the owners of copyright material
reproduced herein and secure permissions, the publishers would like to apologise
for any omissions and will be pleased to incorporate missing acknowledgements
in any future edition of this book.

To Ange, Jemma and Zac, you are the love,
the inspiration and ultimately the turning point.
This book is dedicated to you.

In memory of my grandmother
Joan Eileen Menlove
(1921–1995)

Contents

Acknowledgements

To ACKNOWLEDGE EVERYONE who has played a part in this publication, let alone those characters who have shaped the 39 years of my life so far, is an impossibility, and I apologise to anyone I've left out.

The following people have played an enormous role in helping me write my story and, ultimately, this is as much your book as it is mine.

You guys have made me laugh, kept me focussed, taught me not to be selfish, helped me, loved me and always been honest with me.

Thank you.

First off, my family: Ange, Jemma and Zac; Dad, Mars and Paul; Mum, John, Katherine, Olivia and Stephanie; Judy and Bill.

I would also like to thank Natasha Garnett; Maureen Vincent, Robert Kirby and all at PFD; Sally Potter, Rose

Harrow and all at HarperCollins; everyone at Shanahan; James Sully; Gary Howard and all at Mission; James Maguire; Jonathan Shteinman; Lawrence Lawry; Richard East; Brian Walsh; Brett Goldsmith; Belinda Tainsh; Jan Russ; Mike, Matt and Pete.

And, last but not least, I'd like to say a huge THANK YOU to all those fans who have stuck by me despite the madness.

Introduction

Over the years I have been asked on countless occasions to tell my life story, but I always refused on the grounds that it wasn't the right time for me – and in truth, it wasn't, for I was either too young, too busy or too dazed and confused to be able to make sense of it all. Now that I am a year shy of my fortieth birthday – and thus older and wiser, if a little more weathered – I believe that I am finally in a position to look back and tell my tale as it was. My life to date has been a roller-coaster ride, and at times all I could do was just hang on, but I'm still here and it ain't over yet! As my dad has always said to me, the secret to a long and happy life is not to take it too seriously. You're a long time dead, he says. He's right.

Enjoy!

Chapter One

Searching for Cool

I HAD BEEN excited about the party for some weeks. Who wouldn't be? It's not every day you receive an invitation from Johnny Depp, after all. Okay, so if I'm entirely honest about it, the invitation came by way of a mutual friend, but hey, I was still on the list and they wanted me to come.

The Hollywood star was throwing a party to celebrate the twenty-first birthday of his girlfriend, the supermodel Kate Moss, and he had invited the great and the good – and little old me – to his club, the Viper Room in Los Angeles, to mark the occasion. When the invitation came my way it was an absolute no-brainer for me: there was no way I was going to say no to this one, for I knew that it was going to be the party of all parties.

It was January 1995 and I had flown into LA from Sydney having just completed work on a low-budget Australian movie. I was physically exhausted from the flight but I was in good spirits. After weeks of being on location, working all hours of the day and night, I was excited about the prospect of letting my hair down and having some high-octane fun. Although I didn't know Kate particularly well, we moved within the same circles and had a lot of friends in common, such as the photographer Corinne Day and the hairstylist James Brown, but I was still touched and slightly flattered that I should be included in the revelries. As crowds went, it didn't get much cooler than this: Hollywood stars, supermodels, rock-and-roll legends. Somehow I, a former soap star and pop pin-up, had made the grade.

I checked into my hotel, which was situated right behind the Viper Room, unpacked and took a shower. If I had been sensible I would have got a couple of hours' kip and slept off some of my jetlag, or at the very least had something to eat, but I wasn't in the mood. I had come to LA to party and I wanted it to start right here and now, even though it was the middle of the afternoon. I picked up the telephone and made a call. A friend back home had given me the number of someone who could 'sort me out' and, sure enough, within the hour they were at my hotel door. It was as easy as ringing for a take-out or room service, the only difference being that what they were delivering to me wasn't food or drink – I had called out for drugs.

For a couple of hundred US dollars I purchased a large bag of weed and half an ounce of uncut cocaine. It was more coke than I would have ordered if I had been at home, but I didn't want to risk running out and having to call the dealer again, and in any case the coke in America was half the price of what it was back in Sydney or London.

Once I was alone I drew the curtains of my room, switched on the light and began my well-rehearsed ritual. With a credit card I hacked away at my brick of cocaine until I had enough powder on the surface of the table to cut myself two large lines. With a rolled-up note I snorted them both in quick succession. That initial hit gave me the most intense buzz and at once put paid to my jetlag. I then rolled myself a large joint and, having opened the curtains and the windows, I lay back on my bed and smoked it. It was pure heaven.

Kate's party wasn't until the following evening, and with nothing to do that night I settled into my one-man session. It didn't matter that I didn't have any company – often I found it better that way. When I was high I liked being on my own, in many ways it was much more comforting, more relaxing than being surrounded by people. I'd switch on the television, prop up the pillows on the bed, make myself comfortable, and aimlessly start flicking through the hundreds of channels available on cable. When it got to the point where my thumb started to tire and I could no longer concentrate, I'd get up, move to the nearest table and take out my paper and pens. I'd happily sit there for hours writing lyrics to songs, poems, random thoughts as they came to me. I would start manically sketching in my diary. When I got bored of that I'd take a shower, clean up the room, open the curtains and stare out the window, then shut the curtains again. By the time morning came I would have had no sleep, but that didn't bother me. I was bursting with energy. And in any case, I hadn't come to LA to go to bed, I had come here to have a good time, and as far as I was concerned that's precisely what I was having – a bloody great time.

I'm not exactly sure how I filled that day – all I can remember is that I carried on using. I know that I tried to go out at some stage, but I only made it as far as the news stand because I was feeling slightly paranoid by that point. I was mindful not to overdo the drugs as I wanted to be on form that evening, but I used nevertheless and by the time the party came around I was feeling pretty damn good. Dressed in a pair of tailored hot-pink trousers and a tight Jean Paul Gaultier T-shirt I took a final line and headed off to the club.

Although I had been to LA several times before I had never been to the Viper Room, and the first thing that struck me when I walked through the door was just how small it was. Unlike so many clubs I frequented at that time there was nothing ostentatious about the Viper Room, it was just an intimate venue but it had a very cool, almost Seventies vibe about it. Jotted around a tiny dance floor were small tables, and everywhere you looked was a famous face. Michael Hutchence, who I knew from back home in Australia, was at the party with his girlfriend Helena Christensen, and fellow supermodel Christy Turlington was seated next to her. Thelma Houston was there, as was the designer John Galliano, who had flown in from Paris especially for the night, and then, of course, there were Johnny and Kate, two of the most impossibly beautiful people of their generation. I remember looking around the room and thinking to myself, 'This is the place to be, mate!' Without exception this was the most glamorous and cool party I had ever been to in my life, and I was determined to enjoy every moment of it.

When I left the hotel for the party I decided not to take any drugs with me. The Viper Room had always had something of a wild reputation about it, but after Johnny's friend the actor River Phoenix had collapsed and died outside the club a year earlier, having overdosed on a heroin and cocaine speedball, I didn't think it was wise to start advertising the fact that I had drugs on me. With my hotel just a stone's throw from the club, my plan was to leave my drugs in my room and return there as and when I needed them. It seemed like a good plan at the time, but as the night went on I soon found myself running back and forth like a crazed dog, desperate not to miss a moment of the party yet hungry for my next fix.

By the time midnight came the entire party had hit the dance floor. Gloria Gaynor had just finished singing 'Happy Birthday' to Kate when Johnny and Michael took to the stage. With Johnny on guitar, Michael started to sing the Van Morrison classic 'Gloria' and we were all cheering them on as we danced. The pair were halfway through the song, belting out the chorus, when I realised I was about to go. I knew the symptoms all too well, for it was not the first time this had happened to me. My heart was racing, my vision was blurring, and I was becoming disorientated. I tried to steady myself but there was nothing to grab hold of. I tried to make my way off the dance floor but I had no control over my legs. This is it, I thought, as I started to convulse, this is bloody it, I'm having another seizure – and with that my legs buckled under me and I fell to the floor.

I am not sure what happened in the moments after I fell. When you suffer from seizures you black out and have no recollection of those lost moments in time. What I do know is that someone had pulled the plug on the music, turned the lights on and was calling for an ambulance. A crowd had circled round me and Michael was hovering over me trying to empty my trouser pockets.

'Have you got anything on you?' he kept asking me.

I tried to speak but couldn't.

'It wouldn't be cool if anything was found on you by the medics,' he whispered.

'What are you looking for?' a guest asked him.

'I'm trying to find his wallet,' he lied. 'He'll need his credit card if they take him to hospital.'

'I don't want to go to hospital,' I told James Brown, who was now standing with Michael.

'Jason, for God's sake, you've just fitted – you have to go!'

I must have blacked out again after that, for the next memory I have is of being carried out of the club by the paramedics on a stretcher. I remember that there were paparazzi outside because I could see the flashes of their cameras. 'Who is it?' one of them shouted.

'Never you mind!' belted Michael, who was following me out of the club trying to shield my face from their lenses.

'Is he alive?'

Once again I blacked out.

When I came round the next time I was in the ambulance, and I clearly remember the sound of the siren and thinking how different it was to those back at home in Australia or England. It was like being in some Hollywood cop show. James was at my side. 'You're going to be fine,' he kept telling me. 'Just fine. We just need to get you to hospital and get you looked over.'

I was taken to the Cedars-Sinai and, by coincidence, was seen by an Australian doctor, which for some reason I found vaguely comforting. 'Have you had seizures like this before?' he asked as he took my heart rate.

'A few,' I managed.

'But you have no history of epilepsy?'

'No.'

'I haven't got your toxicology report back yet, but am I right to assume that these seizures are drug-induced?'

I knew that there was no point in lying to him. He'd have his answer soon enough. I nodded.

'Then I suggest that you lay off the drugs from now on. Don't you? You do realise that seizures like this can prove to be fatal. Maybe this will serve as a wake-up call to you.'

It was suggested that I spend the night at the hospital but I refused. I didn't want to spend a moment longer there than I had to, so after three hours I discharged myself and headed back to my hotel by cab. I was so ashamed about what had happened, so racked with guilt that I had ruined Kate's party, that I knew I had to go and apologise to her. She and Johnny were holding an after-party at my hotel, and when I discovered that they were still up I knocked on their door. Johnny answered it.

'I'm really sorry about what happened, mate ...' I ventured.

'That's cool, don't worry,' he said, patting me on the back. 'We're just pleased that you are okay. Now take some advice from me: go to your room, get some sleep, and for God's sake take it easy in future.'

I headed back to my room, tail between my legs. I had made an utter fool of myself. I'd tried to party with the big boys, tried to be so very rock and roll, but all I had done was make a complete fucking idiot of myself. Who was I trying to fool? There was nothing rock and roll about me. I was just a little kid from Melbourne, the boy from *Neighbours* – Scott Robinson with his skateboard, Jason Donovan with his cheesy hits and his teenage fans, Joseph with his Technicolor Dreamcoat. Why couldn't I just accept that and learn to live with myself? What was I constantly trying to prove to others and to myself?

I opened the door to my room, sat down at the table and hung my head in shame. I had just ruined what was possibly one of the greatest nights of my life, and what for?

Drugs.

It was pathetic. I should have listened to Johnny and put my head down and got some rest. I should have taken note of the doctor's words and seen this as my wake-up call, but of course I didn't. Instead, like a moth drawn to a flame, I went over to the drawer of my bedside table and pulled out my stash of cocaine, and without a second thought I cut myself another line.

Chapter Two

Union Street

WHEN I WAS a young boy growing up in Malvern, a leafy suburb of Melbourne, Victoria, I didn't have any desire to become famous. Instead, my ambitions came straight out of the pages of a Boys' Own manual, typical of a generation weaned on a diet of Seventies kids' shows and fads, growing up against a backdrop of Australian sun, surf and sand. At the age of six, as I hung from the lowest branches of the plum tree that stood in our backyard, all I wanted to be when I grew up was Batman, for he was my all-time hero. I'd furiously ride my little bike up and down the Glenferrie Road, near to where we lived, dodging the tram tracks, and imagine that it was my very own Batmobile. When I grew out of that dream, at the age of seven or eight, a fascination with aeroplanes led me to the conclusion that I would one day become a pilot. At the age of nine, having developed a love of water, I saw myself as a swimmer or, better still, a champion surfer. By the time I enrolled at secondary school I wanted to be a graphic artist. In fact, it wasn't until I reached the age of sixteen that I began to entertain the idea of becoming an actor.

And yet, looking back now I can see that it was hardly surprising that I got involved in the world of show business, for, in one form or another, it was very much in my blood. My father, Terence Donovan, was, and still is for that matter, one of Australia's best-loved actors. He took the lead in many stage performances, was a regular star of the small screen, and acted in a number of home-grown movies as well. My mother, Sue Menlove, as she was known before she married Dad, was originally a dancer by profession. She appeared in stage musicals and even enjoyed a stint as a Benny Hill girl in the comedian's eponymous television show. Once she reached the age where it was time for her to hang up her dancing shoes she went on to forge a career as a television presenter, hosting a string of Australian daytime television shows and reading the news.

My parents met in the early Sixties, when Dad had taken a lead role in a production of *West Side Story* and my mother was dancing in *Stop the World – I Want to Get Off*. They met at an after-show party at the Tivoli Theatre in Melbourne, and at first they were nothing more than friends, but as time went on their relationship blossomed into a romance. In 1963, my father, who was on tour in England, appearing at the Oxford Playhouse, rang my mother in Melbourne and proposed to her over the telephone. She accepted and, much to her surprise, received an engagement ring in the post a couple of weeks later. In 1964 my mother travelled over to England by ship and my parents were married in a low-key ceremony in Ashford, Kent. When Dad's run at the Playhouse ended, they set up home just outside Earls Court in London – or Kangaroo Valley as it is affectionately known to all the Aussies who settle there – and stayed there for three years. The house they lived in was situated very close to a railway line and used to shake when the trains rattled past at night, which Dad used to joke may have contributed to my mother getting pregnant with me. When she discovered she was having a baby, my mother was keen to return home to be with her family and friends, and so in 1967 they travelled back to Melbourne, and nine months later, on 1 June 1968, they welcomed into the world their first and only child together – Jason Sean Donovan.

I don't have many recollections of my parents together. I have a hazy picture in my head of holidaying with them in the snow when I can't have been more than three years old, but I can't be sure whether this is a genuine memory or one that I have constructed from an old photograph my father passed on to me. I still, to this day, don't really know why they broke up. Over the years I have toyed with putting this question to both of them, but realise there is little point, for such was the acrimony of their split that with all due respect I doubt very much that either of them would be able to give me a balanced account of what actually happened. All I do know is that one morning, when I was five years old, my mother packed her bags and left.

To say that my mother abandoned me would be too strong. When she walked out of the family home that day I realise now that she wasn't walking away from me but from her marriage. However, as a small child there were times when I didn't see it that way; I couldn't understand why she had left, it was all very confusing. One morning she was there, getting me out of bed, dressing me, making my breakfast, playing with me, and the following day she wasn't and those duties were passed on to Dad like a baton. I must have asked Dad where she had gone to, I must have wanted to know when she was coming back, but I can't remember ever being given an answer to those questions. In later years I would try to piece the jigsaw together, but to this day I am still none the wiser.

To be fair to my mother, initially she did try to make me part of her new life, and not long after she had left and set up home with John McIntosh, a documentary filmmaker whom she later married, I went to stay with them in a house in the village of Sassafras, in the Yarra Ranges. But, try as she might to make me feel at home, I didn't take to it. I felt unsettled and spent most of my time there in tears. I told her at the time it was because I was terrified of the bush fires up there, but if I'm entirely honest about it I was simply homesick and I just wanted to be back where I believed I belonged. The following day, after a conversation with Dad,

13

it was decided that I should return home, and so John drove me back to our house in Union Street, Armadale.

After the events of that weekend my father was adamant that I should live with him full time, and completely dismissed any notion that he and my mother should share joint custody of me. His boy wasn't to be passed from parent to parent, from house to house, like some kind of parcel. I was far too young for that, he argued. At the age of five I needed stability in my life, I needed routine, and now that I have children of my own I can see that he had a point. And so he took my mother to court and fought her for sole custody.

In that day and age, when people were still of the view that a child's place was always with its mother, it was an almost unprecedented move, and as such gained a lot of press coverage at the time, but my father, who was never one to be turned, and still isn't for that matter, stood by his guns and won the case. The judge who presided over the hearing ruled that it was 'in the child's best interest for him to remain with his father in the family home'. I don't know whether my mother was upset by the verdict at the time. According to my father, who understandably always approaches the story with a certain amount of bias, she accepted the situation for what it was and went about her new life. In the years that followed, she and John married and had children of their own – three gorgeous girls: Katherine, Olivia and Stephanie McIntosh.

I was, of course, far too young to know what was going on at the time, but I do remember, a couple of months after

14

Mum left, asking Dad one night when he put me to bed whether they would get back together. But he said nothing, just simply kissed me goodnight.

I still saw my mother from time to time. She didn't live that far away and would always visit me at her mother's house in St Kilda on red-letter days such as birthdays and at Christmas, and I always looked forward to those reunions and would become deeply despondent if for some reason they were ever cancelled.

Children, especially very young ones, are a lot more resilient than adults often care to give them credit for, and as it was I adapted to my new situation with a certain amount of ease. I missed my mother very much in those first few months, but as time went on I learned to channel what feelings I had for her towards my father, and he became the focus of my universe. I still loved my mother very much, but there is no question that the dynamic of our relationship changed. It had to because she wasn't there. She was still my mother, yes, but she wasn't at the school gates in the afternoon, she wasn't at the kitchen table when we sat down for supper, or at my bedside at night. All that fell to Dad. I can't say whether that pained her or not, for it was something that we have never talked about, but I have always consoled myself with the fact that she must have felt something for me.

The sad truth about divorce, especially an acrimonious one, is that it really does tear people apart, and ultimately, as with all battles, there has to be winners and losers. Why my parents couldn't have put their differences behind them for the sake of their child still remains a mystery to me. I would never have expected them to become the best of friends, but to maintain a degree of civility towards one another might have made things a little easier for me as I grew up. However, that wasn't the case, for something happened along the way, something so serious and so dramatic – which I was never privy to – that thirty-five years on they still haven't spoken a single word to one another.

I may have adjusted to the day-to-day routine of life without my mother, but there is no question that her departure left me with emotional scars. As a young boy I was terrified of rejection, and I was deeply insecure and quite emotional. I cried my eyes out during my first day at school, fearing that Dad had left me there for good. At a similar age I was scared of the dark and always slept with the light on, and if Dad was out for the evening I would stay up at night until he returned. I'd lie in my bed, nervously picking away at a hole in the wall I had made, or looking out of the barred window, wondering where he was, when and if he would come home to me, and it was only when I heard the reassuring purr of his car engine as it entered our driveway that I could finally bring myself to go to sleep. If Dad had to go away from home for work, even for a day or two, I would become extremely anxious. I remember being so distraught at school one day when he had left to go on location that my teacher had to call him and ask him to come back, and, like the trooper he was, within an hour he was at the school gates. I realise now that Dad lost out on a lot of career opportunities because of me, and for that I will always be grateful to him.

When Dad took the decision to raise me himself he was well aware that he couldn't do it without help, for at the time he had a regular role on a long-running television police drama called *Division 4*. So it was arranged that his mother, Ethel Arnsby, would come and live with us in Union Street. Dad thought that Ethel might be able to bring a feminine touch to the Donovan household and would act as a kind of surrogate mother to me.

Unlike my mother, who was Australian through and through, Dad was in fact a 'Pom', born and raised in Middlesex, England, who had emigrated to Australia with his brothers in their twenties, in search of a better life. They had settled at a place called Sunshine, in Melbourne, and shortly afterwards my grandmother followed them out there.

Despite living in Australia for many years, Ethel had never lost touch with her roots back home, and she liked to regale me with stories of my Anglo-Irish ancestors in her strong London accent, which seemed quite alien to me as a young boy. There was the tale of how the Arnsbys and the Donovans had been the last licensed cow-herders of Kensington, which still amuses me to this day as I now live not far from where they set up shop in Notting Hill – or Notting Dale, as it was known then – and Ethel liked to talk about the war and explain what it was like bringing up four sons during the Blitz. I remember she wore orthopaedic boots, that the only meal she ever seemed to cook for Dad and me was egg and chips or the occasional roast, and that she forecast the weather through her feet, which is something of a Donovan trait. I also remember trying to steal the loose change from her purse when she wasn't looking. It was hardly a conventional set-up. An eighty-year-old woman, a forty-something man and a five-year-old boy all living under the same roof, but somehow we muddled along.

Though she was always there for me when I needed her, I think it would be fair to say that Ethel was at an age where she couldn't really cope with me on her own, and so when I finished school in the afternoon I would always join Dad on the set of *Division 4* if he was still filming. Crawfords, the production company that made the series, were sympathetic to Dad's predicament and made every effort to accommodate me while I was there with him. In many ways they became my second family, and the studio became my second home. I would while away my time after school playing in the trailers and mucking around with production crew.

Shortly after his divorce came through, Dad started dating a woman called Heather McLaren, who worked as a wardrobe mistress at Crawfords. Heather was an incredible person, both warm and affectionate, and she and I got on well. Although she never came to live with us, for a time she played a major role in my life. Sometimes, if she had a moment free from the studio, she would pick me up from school and would take me back to the costume trailer at the studios, where she would sit and play with me until Dad had finished work. On other occasions, on the proviso that I would be well-behaved and quiet, she would take me to see Dad on set, which I always found exciting.

One of my earliest memories is of watching a scene shot at a railway station. The cameras were on one side of the track, and for some reason I was on the other, and so the crew called me over to their side so that I wouldn't be in the frame – but even though it was obviously a set and the trains they were using in the shoot were stationary and were never going to move, I remember being too scared to run over the track in case one of the trains hit me, so I walked the whole way round. Another memory I have is of Dad letting me ride in his police car while he was filming. He'd put me on the back seat and cover me with a blanket so that I couldn't be seen and he'd drive off. It was a great thrill and I particularly liked it when he was involved in a car chase. If Dad knocked off from filming early and was able to collect me from school he'd be in such a rush to make it on time that invariably he'd turn up in costume. He'd be there at the gates in his shirtsleeves with his fake, welded gun stashed in his holster, which I always thought was pretty cool.

It can't have been easy for Dad, trying to juggle his life as an actor with being a single parent, but he did his best and what free time he had was devoted solely to me. He would take me swimming to the local baths and to the beach; he taught me to play tennis and helped me with my school-work. He encouraged me to love music, insisting that I took piano classes and joined the local choir, and when I was older he passed on his entire collection of Beatles records to me, which was one of the greatest gifts he could have given me. And I loved him for all of that, he was without a doubt my hero and could do no wrong in my eyes.

The only area where Dad was lacking as a parent was on the domestic front. Not only was the Donovan household chaotic to say the least, but when it came to the kitchen Dad was a complete philistine, and for the first few years of my life I lived on a diet that would have left the likes of Jamie Oliver or Donna Hay reeling. It was egg and chips for lunch, and egg and chips for supper. I can't remember ever being given anything green to eat in that house, other than Ethel's soggy Brussels sprouts, which were inedible as it was, and by the age of nine I was so sick of the sight of fried eggs and those oven-baked chips that I taught myself how to cook an omelette. For my packed lunch at school Dad would prepare me one of his legendary jam sandwiches, which, to put it politely, were completely bloody inedible. Two thick slabs of white crusty bread, which were usually so stale that if you threw them to the ground they would smash like porcelain, covered in a layer of fluorescent-pink Blue Brand jam, for such was Dad's frugality that everything in our larder had to be economy. (To this day I still approach Dad's store cupboard and fridge with a degree of trepidation, for I know that ninety per cent of its contents will be well beyond its use-by date.) Dad would proudly present my lunch to me in its paper bag as I left for school each morning, with such a sense of flourish that you would have thought he had just spent hours knocking up a cordon bleu banquet, and reluctantly I would take it from him, promising to eat every last morsel of it. At break-time I would look longingly at my classmates' lunch boxes filled with pieces of fruit and other treats as I unwrapped my sorry little package. I sometimes think that our poodle, Abby, ate better than we did in those days.

As determined as my father was to raise me single-handedly, he was aware that as a young boy I needed to have some female influence in my life. Although I got on well with Ethel and had come to form a bond with Heather, Dad knew that this wasn't enough. He could see that Ethel was becoming increasingly frail and couldn't really relate to a boy of my age, and although Dad's relationship with Heather was strong at the time, I think he was aware of the fact that unless their relationship became more permanent he couldn't expect her to step into my mother's shoes. And so he encouraged me to form a close bond with my maternal grandmother, Joan Menlove, who lived not far from us in the suburb of St Kilda. Joan, or Gran as I called her, was everything to me and I loved every moment I spent with her.

In many ways Gran was more like a mother to me than a grandmother. Unlike Ethel, who always seemed so very old, Gran was vibrant and quite active for her age and she provided me with a sense of love and security. When Dad's work took him out of town I would be sent to stay with her, and at weekends as a treat she would put me up. It was a world away from anything I knew. There'd be freshly baked cakes on the table at teatime, roasts at the weekend, and if I

was lucky she would cook me my favourite of all her dishes
– chow mein. I'd be put to bed at night in her spare room,
where the beds were so old that they sloped in the middle,
and she'd cover me in blankets, propping the soft down
pillows under my head before she kissed me goodnight. In
the morning she would wake me with a cup of tea, laced
with two and a half teaspoonfuls of sugar, and then we'd be
off and out on one of her adventures. She'd take me for
walks down to the markets to buy ingredients for one of her
feasts, and if I was really lucky we would go up country to
Millgrove, Warburton, to the little house she shared with
her boyfriend, Jim.

Every year, as a special treat, Gran would take me to the
Royal Melbourne Show. She would make us a picnic of
chicken sandwiches and a flask of tea, and we would go off
to watch the cow parade together in the main stand, picking
up show bags of sweets, toys and souvenirs as we passed all
the stands. When I was old enough I'd take the tram from
school to the Freemasons' Hospital, where she worked as a
receptionist, and after she had clocked off for the day we
would go back to her house for the weekend. I would take
my bike up there and spend my afternoons collecting
tadpoles or swinging over the Yarra River on a rope when
the weather was good.

But it wasn't just my grandmother's cooking or her sense
of homeliness that made me want to be with her. Right from
the beginning there was a deep connection between us.
Maybe it had something to do with the fact that I was her

first grandchild, or maybe she felt responsible for me in some way after Mum had left, but she was always there for me. I felt I could tell her anything, no matter how silly or trivial it was, and there was nothing I liked more than chatting to her as she smoked her way through her trusty packet of Peter Stuyvesant reds, which she never seemed to be without. If Gran was unhappy about the way things had turned out between my mother and father, she never let on to me. She took it upon herself to act as a go-between for my parents and tried to protect me from their feud. All the meetings that I had with my mother over those years were always staged at my grandmother's house, and later on when my sisters were born she encouraged us to form a relationship, which exists to this day.

Throughout my childhood and teenage years Gran tried to give me a sense of stability and security that was lacking in my life. She was determined that I would not suffer as a result of what had happened between my parents, and was always at hand to give me the love and sense of belonging that I so desperately craved and needed as a young boy.

Chapter Three

Kilowatt Smile

As a small boy it never really occurred to me that Dad's career was anything out of the ordinary. I guess I just assumed that all fathers dressed up as policemen for a living and spent their days solving pretend crimes. It wasn't until I was about six or seven that I became conscious of the fact that my dad was slightly different from those of my friends. If we went out for a walk or took a trip to the shops, people would stop and stare at him in the street, and sometimes the more courageous of them would come over and ask him for an autograph, which I always thought was a bit strange.

'Why do they want *your* autograph?' I'd asked him once when a fan came up to him in our local butcher's shop.

'I've got absolutely no idea!' he'd laughed.

At school break-time the kids would talk about seeing him on the television the night before, and if he came to collect me in the afternoon they would flock round him. For some reason this always unsettled me, and I would find myself almost protectively clinging to his leg as we walked off, as if to make it blatantly clear to my friends that he was *mine* and not theirs, something that my own daughter, Jemma, who is at a similar age, does with me today!

And yet even though Dad was relatively successful and well-known, there was absolutely nothing remotely starry or luvvie about him. Passionate as he was for his craft, he had no airs and graces and was refreshingly down to earth about his profession. He wasn't in it for the fame or the money, Dad acted because he wanted to, because he was good at it, and because he had the opportunity to do so. When people asked him what it was like being an actor he'd just shrug. 'It's nice work *when* you can get it,' he'd say with a grin. Maybe it was something to do with his working-class background or perhaps the fact that for so many years he had slaved away at a succession of menial jobs and factory work before he was given his first break, but Dad never took what he did for granted. He was a grafter through and through. 'Never be ashamed to work hard,' he'd tell me. 'You'll only get where you want to be in life if you put in the hours.'

He was the same when it came to money. Dad was rarely out of work and had earned a tidy sum thanks to his six-year stint on *Division 4*, but you would never have known it to look at him. Our house on Union Street was a normal suburban Australian family home. There were no flash cars in the driveway, no fancy furnishings, tennis courts or swimming pools. Dad abhorred ostentation and preferred to live a simple life. He wasn't into designer clothes, posh restaurants or taking exotic holidays. He didn't have time for the champagne lifestyle that went hand in hand with his job. He was happiest at home with his plate of egg and chips and a couple of cold tins of beer from the fridge (although his tastes have moved on a little since then).

If I'm completely honest about it – and I have said this to his face so I'm sure he won't have a problem with me putting this in print – Dad was a bit of a bloody tight arse! And yet, to give him his dues, I can understand why. My father had come from nothing and was determined not to go back to that, and he was also acutely aware of just how precarious life as an actor can be, always treating every paycheque as though it was his last. He was forever squirreling money away, saving it for those rainy days or the times when he was out of work, or 'resting' as they say in the business.

From the earliest age Dad always impressed upon me the importance of gaining a good education. As a child of wartime Britain and its aftermath it was something that he had missed out on himself, and he was determined that I should make the best of my schooldays. He didn't expect me to come top of my class, he didn't stand over me when I did my homework, he simply wanted me to always try to do my best – not for his sake but for my own.

I took his words on board, and while I was not the most academic child in the world I always worked hard and took my studies seriously. But, as keen as Dad was for me to get the best education I could, what amuses me to this day is that even though he could have afforded it he was never prepared to go the whole nine yards and dip into his pockets to privately school me. After kindergarten I was sent to the local state primary, Spring Road School, and when my time there drew to an end Dad put me down for De La Salle, a Catholic college in the area, known for its academic and sporting achievements. There was just one hitch to Dad's master plan: I wasn't a Catholic.

'Don't think I haven't thought of that,' Dad exclaimed when the topic came up over dinner one night. 'You can convert! You've got Irish blood in you, which I'm sure counts for something.' And so, at the age of twelve I was marched down to the local church one Sunday morning and was baptised. Anything to save a dollar or two.

As it was I didn't have any real objection to Dad's plan, nor to my conversion for that matter. I had my heart set on De La Salle from the moment I'd learned that Anthony Catrice was going there, and was happy to go along with Dad's ruse if it meant securing a place. Anthony was my best friend at the time and we were practically joined at the hip. Not only did he live close by to me, but we were in the same year at Spring Road. In our free time we would race our bikes up and down Union Street and hang out together on the steps of the Salvation Army building next to our house, and at weekends we attended music class at the Melbourne Conservatorium – he took violin lessons, while I took piano.

A year before I took my place at De La Salle I was offered my first acting role. Crawfords, the company that had produced *Division 4*, were looking for an eleven-year-old boy to take a guest role in their lunchtime airport serial *Skyways*. Dad's run with *Division 4* had come to an end in the mid-Seventies, but after a five-year sabbatical from the small screen, during which time he had returned to the stage and taken on a number of small film roles, he had returned to the fold and was now starring in their primetime show *Cop Shop*. A producer at Crawfords asked Dad one afternoon whether I would be interested in the role. At that stage my acting experience was limited to the odd brief appearance in my primary-school plays, but that didn't matter to the people at Crawfords. As far as they were concerned, having known me since I was a little boy and seen me recently on set with Dad, I was what they were looking for.

Dad understandably had his reservations. Although he was not completely immune to the idea of me following in his footsteps – if that was what I really wanted in life – he was determined I would complete my education first, so that if things didn't work out for me in the future I would at least have something to fall back on. But when he heard that it was only a couple of days' work and that the filming schedule was such that I wouldn't miss too much school, he started to come round to the idea. I think he felt that it was an experience I might learn from and that it might give me a degree of confidence and self-awareness, which I was perhaps lacking back then.

I didn't have any interest in following Dad into acting at the time, but when he told me that, as well as taking two days off school, I'd be paid for the job, I leapt at the chance. 'You're not keeping the money, though, I'll put it aside for you,' he said. He opened an account for me at the local State bank, depositing my $300 fee and my expenses.

My memories of the first few days are quite vague. I remember being driven to Melbourne airport where we were filming on location, which I thought was pretty cool as it was, and of spending time in the morning in a trailer, desperately trying to memorise the couple of lines I had been given as I was fitted into costume. Later that morning the director introduced me to a girl who looked pretty much the same age as me, and told me that she would be playing my on-screen sister.

'Done this before?' she asked as we headed out of the trailer onto the set.

'No. Have you?'

'A bit here and there,' she replied with a little smile. 'What's your name then?'

'Jason Donovan,' I blurted. 'What's yours?'

'Kylie – Kylie Minogue.'

I enjoyed my two days' work on *Skyways* and Kylie seemed nice enough. She was pretty chirpy and friendly and we had a laugh together running around the airport pretending to be lost, looking for our parents, but after filming was wrapped and we said our goodbyes I didn't give her a second thought. I was far too young to be interested in girls, and if anything I remember thinking she was a little skinny.

Despite my lack of experience, Crawfords were happy with my performance, and in the next few years a number of small roles followed. In 1980 I took a part in the children's television series called *I Can Jump Puddles*, based on Alan Marshall's story of his battle against polio, and made guest appearances in a further two dramas – *Home*, and *Golden Pennies*.

Apart from wanting me to succeed at school, Dad wasn't much of a disciplinarian, and for the most part my childhood was what I would describe as pretty 'free range'. So long as I was polite, respectful of others, turned up for meals and went to bed at a reasonable hour, I was my own agent. Having been an insecure younger child, by the time I reached the age of eleven I had become quite independent. Ethel had passed away a couple of years before, and Dad's relationship with Heather had come to an end, and so it was now just Dad and me living together in Union Street. I look back on those years nowadays and I sometimes think we were more like a couple of flatmates than we were father and son. When I got home from school, having completed my homework I'd play music loudly in my room, while Dad would sit around the house with his theatrical mates, drinking beer and wine, getting increasingly raucous. Sometimes when I was bored I would climb up the jacaranda tree at the back of the house, using its branches like the steps of a ladder, until I reached the top of our garden shed, and I would sit there on the hot tin roof, basking in the Australian sun, and teach myself how to smoke. I would roll up pieces of card and light them up and puff away at the smouldering paper until my fingers burned, or I'd slip the odd Stuyvie from Gran's packet when she wasn't looking and practise my technique on them.

Although my childhood wasn't as conventional as those of my friends, I was pretty happy with my lot. I could always retreat to Gran's when I wanted some home comfort, and on the whole I reckoned that Dad and I made a pretty good team. But in the summer of 1979, shortly after my stint on *Skyways*, all that suddenly changed.

Since his relationship with Heather had come to an end, Dad had dated a couple of women. They came over to the house and would be introduced to me, but Dad never referred to them as anything more than friends and they certainly didn't stay over. But when he met Marlene it was a different story. I knew from the moment Dad introduced me to her that this time it was serious. The look on his face said it all as he proudly showed her off to me. He was in love.

Marlene Saunders was one of the most glamorous women I had ever set eyes on. She was tall and thin, with a mane of thick brown hair that tumbled over her shoulders, and had this kilowatt smile that could stop you dead in your tracks, so I wasn't surprised to learn that she was a model. Her face and figure had graced the cover of countless magazines, such as *Cosmo* and *Vogue*, as well as billboard campaigns, and she had appeared in a number of television commercials as well. She and my father had met at a party through mutual friends, the Australian actor Tony Bonner, who had worked alongside Dad in both *Division 4* and *Cop Shop*, and his wife Nola Bonner. Looks apart, it was easy to see what Dad saw in Marlene. As well as having a sharp mind, she was easy-going and had a great sense of humour. Quite what attracted her to my father was less obvious to me, although I remember her telling me later on that she found him one of the most charming men she had ever met.

Marlene made an effort with me right from the start. She was warm and friendly, good-natured and fun to be around. She never patronised me but talked to me like an adult. I couldn't help but like her from the outset, and that's what troubled me – for there was a part of me that really, really wanted to hate her. It almost pains me to write this now, for over the years my relationship with Marlene has become one of the most important ones of my life, but that's how I felt at the time. I'd lie in bed at night, and as I listened to her and Dad through the walls, chatting away and laughing, I'd wish that she would just go away. I wanted her out of our lives and for things to go back to how they were before.

It all seems so childish to me now, but I suppose I was just terrified that Marlene was taking Dad away from me. Since Mum had left I had effectively had him all to myself, and I liked it that way. For a time Heather had been a part of our lives, but I never once felt that I had to share Dad with her. With that relationship there had been boundaries, for she had never lived with us, she didn't intrude into our lives in any way, she was there in the background. Now that I was older and understood more about relationships, I saw Marlene as a threat. My father was clearly besotted with her and that frightened me. I guess the legacy of my mother's departure still cast a shadow over me. I may have thought that I was so very independent, but inside I was still emotionally insecure and extremely sensitive, and I was still too young to realise that it was possible for Dad to love two people at once.

When Marlene first came to live with us I admit that I didn't make life very easy for her. I was prone to tantrums and would take my moods out on her, which was very uncharacteristic of me. Although I never articulated my fears to Gran, she picked up on them, and when she tentatively broached the subject with me I thought that in her I would have an ally.

'Don't you want your father to be happy?' she asked me.

'Yes, of course, but ...'

She cut me off. There were to be no 'buts' with Gran when it came to Marlene, for, like everyone else who came into contact with her, Gran adored Dad's new girlfriend.

'Give it some time, Jason. You'll get used to it and come round in the end.'

And, of course, as always, Gran was right. After a couple of months I melted and the barriers came down. I could see

Marlene was making Dad happy and I learned to understand that his feelings for her didn't compromise his love for me in any way. And, in any case, I soon realised that it was nice having a woman in our lives. Almost overnight, Dad and I stopped living like a couple of unruly bachelors. The Donovan household had a new feeling about it. It was certainly a lot cleaner and more comfortable than it had been before, and Marlene quickly weaned Dad off his diet of egg and chips, much to my relief, and started cooking roasts, curries, Italian dishes and my favourite salmon mousse for us. She may not have been able to cure Dad of his parsimony, but one thing was for sure: when she was doing the shopping, she never went Blue Brand. Marlene was quality through and through.

One of the first things Marlene did when she moved in with us was to help me decorate my bedroom. Though it had never occurred to me that my room needed a makeover, to her it looked like a spare room, almost cell-like, she would say. There was nothing in that room to suggest that a young boy lived there. The walls were bare, the shelves were empty.

'Don't you want to stamp your identity on this room?' she asked me one day.

'How?'

She raised an eyebrow. 'I'll show you.'

That afternoon Marlene and I went shopping and bought a selection of posters of my favourite bands at the time – the Beatles and Kiss. She even bought me a new doona or duvet,

34

as they say in the UK, when she realised just how limp and empty my old one was.

What I liked about Marlene the most was that she was straight up. Although she was fully aware of what had happened between my parents, and was sensitive about the effect their split had had on me, she made it clear that she had no intention of trying to fill my mother's shoes or replace her in any way. All she wanted was for us to be friends, and I was happy about that. Marlene was only thirty-two when she walked into my life, and although I always felt close to Dad, in many ways she bridged the gap between us. Just as with Gran, I felt I could talk to Marlene about anything and would always go to her with my problems.

A year after they first started seeing each other, Dad and Marlene decided to marry. I know that they were nervous about telling me but they shouldn't have been, because I was completely made-up and deeply honoured when Dad asked me to be his best man. On the day of the wedding, which was held at home, I remember turning to Marlene and asking her what I would call her now she was my step-mother.

'Well, what do you reckon? Why don't you call me Marls – that's what my friends call me, after all?'

I never called Marlene Marls. Instead I came up with my own name for her – Mars. I guess, subconsciously, I was looking for a name that came as close to 'Ma' as I could find.

Chapter Four

No.6 Tram

I WAS FOURTEEN years old when Marlene gave birth to my brother Paul. I know that both she and Dad were concerned about how I would react to the new arrival in our house, having effectively been an only child for so many years, but I was really pleased to have a younger brother. Marlene was the most fantastic stepmother and couldn't have been kinder or more loving to me; but I knew that she desperately wanted a child of her own. The day she returned from the hospital with Paul in her arms I remember feeling that at last I was part of a proper, functional family.

I was in my second year at De La Salle and had settled in well. It was quite obvious that I would never become a rocket scientist – I was relegated to the veggie maths group in my first term there – but I kept up with my studies and continued to do my best. I found that so long as my subjects didn't require too much analysis then I was fine. I had a good memory and discovered that I could take in quite a lot of information fairly quickly and retain it, which would, of course, come to serve me well in later life. Politics, economics and accountancy were all subjects that I did well in, but the class I enjoyed the most was without a doubt art. I loved drawing and found that I had a natural flair for it.

Although I was never part of the really cool gang at school – the boys with their New Romantic haircuts and winklepicker shoes – I had a good circle of friends and was close to a lot of the older boys. Having wanted to go to De La Salle because I couldn't countenance the notion of being parted from Anthony Catrice, I soon found that we had drifted apart, as children often do. We were still mates, we always would be, but as we grew up we started to move with different crowds. But I wasn't too bothered about that, for I had a new partner to spar with – the irrepressible Mr James McGuire (or Maggot, as he was nicknamed). It would be fair to say that James and I were a little wary of each other to start with, but within a couple of months the barriers came down, and when it soon became clear that we shared the same pursuits in life, namely surfing and girls, that was it, we were friends for life.

James and I spent our teenage years living in each other's pockets. We were completely inseparable. If he wasn't round at my house, then I was at his. It got to the point where if Dad came home in the evening and found me on my own, his first question would be 'Where's Jamo?' When we weren't holed up in my bedroom listening to music then we would be down at the beach, looking for waves and, of course, the girls.

I may have been a conscientious student but I was no saint. To my father's horror and Marlene's amusement I had my ear pierced around this time, and also took up smoking, which infuriated Dad as I would openly light up in front of him. Dad liked the odd cigarette from time to time, but he was never a real smoker, it was simply something he did after a couple of drinks. He'd have a few, nab a fag from a friend and light up, and you know what, he looked absolutely bloody ridiculous! Dad had mastered a lot of tricks as an actor but smoking wasn't one of them. He'd sit there waving his fag around as he talked, pouting and puffing away but never inhaling. So when I took up smoking I decided to be quite professional about it, and to follow Gran's lead rather than my father's. Twenty a day, red Stuyvies – it was always all or nothing with me. When Dad found out he was furious and banned me from smoking in the house, so to avoid his wrath I'd take my habit up to the shed roof and puff away while I spied on the couple next door, who, to my great enjoyment, had a habit of sunbathing naked.

A lot of my friends at that age had started experimenting with alcohol. They'd sneak tins of beer into school to drink at the back of the bike sheds after class, and invariably there would be a bottle of spirits or sickly liqueur, stolen from some parents' drinks table, doing the rounds at the parties we went to. But I wasn't into that. It wasn't the smell or even the taste of alcohol that put me off, I just hated the idea of what it did to you. Although my father was by no means a heavy drinker, he liked his beer and wine and there had been times during my childhood when I had seen him a little worse for wear. He could get loud and rowdy when he'd had a few, he'd become quite forthright and a tad belligerent or even aggressive (something my mother had mentioned as a possible reason for their break-up). I never liked seeing him that way, simply because it went against his very nature. So I steered well away from the lure of the bottle, and throughout my teenage years and young adult-hood I never touched a drop of the stuff – not even a beer. But as immune as I was to drink, I didn't live a life of total abstinence, for I had my own little poison – dope.

I can't have been much older than fourteen when I smoked my first joint. I guess it was just a natural progression from the killer weed, i.e. nicotine. It's just part and parcel of the teenage rite of passage. One day you're out there behind the bike shed sharing a fag with your friends; the next you're tugging away on your first doobie. From the moment I tried my first spliff I got a taste for it. I liked the way it made me feel – happy and full of laughter. Unlike alcohol, which in my mind back then seemed to mar the senses, dope – be it hash or grass – was a very sensuous drug. You only had to have a couple of puffs on a joint for the world to become a much brighter, more beautiful place.

Although I'd always partake of a joint if it was offered to me, it wasn't until I was in my mid-teens that I started to buy my own. It was quite easy to come by in Melbourne at that time, and so with what pocket money I had I'd go into town and score my little bag of grass. I wouldn't buy very much, just enough for a couple of joints, and I would keep my little stash in a box, which I hid in my bedroom. Sometimes after school, when I had finished my homework, I'd roll myself a tiny joint and have a few puffs on it, and then I would sit there and doodle away on my sketch pad, listening to my record collection, or I'd strum away on my guitar, for I found that smoking weed got my creative juices flowing. And there was nothing I liked more than to wake up on a Saturday morning and have a little puff before I headed off to the coast, surfing with James.

For a time, Dad was completely oblivious to my little habit. In the early Eighties we had moved into the next-door house because we needed more space, and my new bedroom was in a self-contained bungalow at the back of the property, but when I did finally get rumbled he wasn't pleased. Unlike Marlene, whose take on drugs was fairly liberal having been on the scene during the Seventies, Dad was of a generation that hadn't come into much contact with drugs, and as such regarded any drug, be it hard or soft, as 'evil'.

'I just don't understand why you kids want to do this to yourselves. You'll end up as an addict, you know.'

'Oh come on, Terry,' Marlene would say. 'It's just a little pot. All kids his age do it. It's really not a big deal.'

'I just don't want him to throw his life away, that's all. You read about this kind of thing in the papers every day. It's terrifying.'

If he caught me smoking a joint in my room with a friend, he would go mad. 'You bloody pot heads! It smells like an opium den in here!'

As it was, Dad needn't have worried. As much as I enjoyed getting stoned now and again, I still only used occasionally and I certainly never let it interfere with my schoolwork. At the age of sixteen I had decided that I wanted to be a graphic artist and was looking into enrolling at the Royal Melbourne Institute of Technology when I finished school. I'd do a foundation course, then specialise, and once I had graduated I'd join a firm, maybe in Melbourne or Sydney even. I had it all mapped out, or thought I did at least, for at the beginning of 1985 I received a phone call from my father's agent, Gary Stewart, that made me rethink my career altogether.

A television production company called Grundy's was casting for a new teatime soap opera called *Neighbours*, which was to be launched on Australia's Channel Seven early that year. Set in a fictional suburban cul de sac, the series was to follow the lives of the families who lived there. The producers were looking for a boy of my age to play the part of Danny Ramsay, and they wanted to know whether I was interested. It had been quite a while since I had been in anything, and although I still didn't harbour any ambitions to become an actor I was flattered that they had thought of me, so I agreed to come in to the studios and audition for the part with a casting agent called Jan Russ. I remember feeling quite nervous as I took the number six tram from the corner of the High Street to the studios on Prahran. I'd come straight from school and was in my uniform. When I asked Dad whether I should change for the audition he told me not to. 'Go as you are and just be yourself,' he had said. 'My attitude is never overdo it, just look clean, tidy and respectable.' My school uniform was probably the smartest thing I had in my wardrobe at that time, but unfortunately by the time I got to the audition it was anything but. There were ink stains on my cuffs, grass stains on my knees, I hadn't combed my hair and I'd been in such a rush to get there I had completely forgotten to tighten my tie. When I was introduced to Jan she took one look at me and just laughed. I thought I must have blown it but she put me at ease, and as I began to read for her I could tell that she had warmed to me because she had this big smile on her face.

A couple of days later my agent Gary Stewart called me at home.

'Well, did you get it?' asked Dad as I put down the telephone.

'Yes, I did.'

'That's great,' said Marlene.

'It is and it isn't – the contract is for a whole year.'

'And?'

'Well, it would mean I'd have to drop out of school.'

In the days that followed I thought long and hard about what I should do, and it was a tough call. If I dropped out of school then I would be kissing away my education, all those years of hard work. If things didn't work out I could always return and complete my HSC later on, but I knew in my heart of hearts that it was really unlikely I would do that. On the other hand, if I stayed on at school and said no to the role then maybe I was turning down the greatest opportunity of my life. The part paid well and was guaranteed for at least a year. Surely it would lead to other things in the future?

When I asked my teachers what I should do, much to my surprise, they almost unanimously told me to go for the part. Kevin Burke, my English teacher at the time, told me that he thought I could make it as an actor. I had impressed him earlier that year with a reading from Peter Shaffer's play *Equus*, so much so that he had even gone so far as to say that he could see me on *Parkinson* one day, which I think was going a bit too far! My friends thought I should go for it too.

Faced with this almost impossible dilemma I turned to Dad for his advice, for I realised he was the one person I could trust on this matter. I knew he was proud that I had landed the role – no doubt feeling pleased that his son had turned out to be a bit of a chip off the old block – but I also knew his views on education.

'I think you know what I'm going to say, Jason – stay at school. If this is meant to happen then it will, and I'm sure that if you have got this far then there will be other opportunities for you in the future, but for now I'd get on with your studies. You've come this far and it would be such a waste for you to throw it all away at this stage.'

I heard what he was saying and trusted his judgement. The offer had been tempting – I was, after all, being handed this brilliant opportunity on a plate – but I couldn't do it. I knew I had to complete my education and get my HSC. Dad had been lucky with his career but it hadn't always been a walk in the park. I remember as though it was yesterday the moment he told me that his character had been axed from *Cop Shop*, and even though he quickly got other work I will never forget the worry etched on his face in the days that followed. I'd seen a lot of Dad's friends, who were just as talented as he was, really struggle too. Working in this business definitely increases any feelings of insecurity you might already have. While they worked solidly during their twenties and thirties, when they hit middle age they suddenly found that the phone stopped ringing and they were forced to reconsider their careers. My mind was made up. I had to get my school certificate, and so later that afternoon I called the production company and told them my decision.

As it transpired my choice turned out to be the right one, for as I entered my final year at school (Year 12), Dad came back from work one day to tell me that Channel Seven had decided to drop *Neighbours* from its schedule. Although there was nothing wrong with the show itself – I'd watched a couple of episodes out of curiosity when it launched and I liked it – the ratings had been poor so they had decided to pull the plug on it. I couldn't help but feel a huge sense of relief.

I spent the rest of the year with my head in a book getting ready for my exams. I'd put in all my paperwork to enrol on the graphic design course at RMIT, and although I was still smoking cigarettes, I had even gone so far as to give up weed so I could concentrate on my studies. It was September and I was just about to embark on my Swot Vac, the month-long revision sabbatical Australian schools give you before your HSC. I was heading off to stay with Gran in Frankston so I could study in peace and was busy packing up my textbooks and a large carton of ciggies when the phone rang. It was Gary, Dad's agent. I assumed he wanted to speak to Dad and was about to call him when Gary said it was me he wanted to talk to.

'How do you fancy auditioning for *Neighbours* again?' he asked.

I thought that Gary must have lost his mind for a moment. 'Hasn't it been axed?'

'No, it's coming back onto our screens again. Channel Ten has just re-commissioned it and they are completely revamping the show. New cast, new characters, new scripts. And guess what? They want you.'

'But I'm in the middle of my exams.' Why did these breaks always seem to come up at the most inopportune of times?

'No problem. It doesn't start filming until the end of the year. If you want the part I'd say it's pretty much yours, and it's a great role. They want you to play this kid called Scott Robinson – sounds quite fun to me. I know it's short notice but do you want to come in and audition today?'

What's the harm in trying, I thought, and so as soon as I hung up the telephone I jumped on the train back to Malvern, hopped on my bike and peddled up to Grundy's for another audition with Jan. Two days later, when I was back up in Frankston, the call came in. It was Gary.

'It's a yes, Jason.'

'Really?'

'Yes, I've just had them on the phone. They wanted to check to see whether you would be able to start towards the end of the year. So come on, Jason, tell me ... are you interested or not?'

Chapter Five

Ramsay Street

I COULDN'T HELP but feel slightly nervous as I made my way to Channel Ten's studios in Nunawading, in the eastern suburbs of Melbourne, for my first day of filming in November 1985. I had some acting experience under my belt, but I had never really considered those brief and sporadic appearances on TV to be anything more than a bit of fun. I was just a kid 'play acting' my way through a succession of minor roles that were incidental to the main action of the plot. If I fluffed my lines, if my performance wasn't quite up to scratch, it was of little consequence for I was never on screen long enough for anyone to notice. Back then I was nothing more than Terry Donovan's son, farmed out to studios by way of a favour because certain productions required a boy of roughly my age, height and appearance to fill a role. But now, as I stood on the set of *Neighbours* for the first time and got my bearings, I realised the enormity of what I had committed myself to. I was no longer just my father's son, I was an actor in my own right, and I suddenly understood that from the moment I had put my name on the contract I had signed away a year of my life to the soap. So it wasn't Shakespeare, but it was a start.

As soon as Gary had rung to tell me I had the part I'd known I had to accept, for fortune doesn't always knock twice at your door. After I'd given him my answer the first person I called was Dad. He was over the moon for me. 'I told you patience pays off! We'll celebrate properly once your exams are over, but for now just get back to the books, you hear me?'

As hard as it was I did just that, for having come this far with my education I didn't want to bail out now. I was always very determined like that, and even though I had the security of a job waiting for me, I still wanted to prove myself and rise to the challenge.

And so, once I put the telephone down, I walked into Gran's kitchen and brewed myself a cup of strong tea before heading off into the garden to the makeshift workstation I had set up in her shed. I took a deep breath, lit up a Stuyvie, opened my textbook and knuckled down to my revision.

There wasn't time to take much of a break following my final exam, for within a couple of weeks my first batch of scripts had arrived at Union Street. I opened the package with a degree of trepidation. Having been briefed by the production company on the gist of what the show was about and who my character was, it all seemed rather daunting. There looked to be so much work to do before I even got on set, for I had to familiarise myself with the storyline as a whole, as well as get to grips with my own character and his scenes. There were a lot of established and respected actors within the cast. What if I let them all down; what if I messed up? I knew I could act, I'd been told as much before by the directors I'd worked with in the past, and even Jan had told me that she thought I was good during my auditions, but I couldn't help but feel nervous. Maybe I had bitten off more than I could chew.

'Don't be so ridiculous!' Dad would say when I voiced my fears to him.

'If you weren't any good they wouldn't have taken you on. These people are professionals and they know what they are doing. My only advice is to work hard. Always be prepared, get those lines under your belt until they come so naturally to you that you don't even have to think twice about them. That's when you start really acting.' And so, with that in mind, I locked myself away in my bedroom and read those scripts over and over again as though my life depended on it. I'd get out my sketchbook and work each scene out step by step, following the stage directions. I was determined not to make any mistakes.

As it turned out, my first day went reasonably well and the cast and crew could not have been more welcoming. In my first scene I was lying in bed in the St Agnes Memorial Hospital. My character had ended up there after he had been mugged as he tried to run away from home. It wasn't

49

exactly very arduous work, as all I had to do was just lie there.

The premise of the soap was to follow the comings and goings of four families of neighbours who lived together in a modern cul-de-sac, called Ramsay Street, in the fictional suburb of Erinsborough. Among the characters who were central to the storyline was the plumber Max Ramsay, whose forefathers, according to *Neighbours* lore, had founded and named the street. Max, who was played by the actor Francis Bell, lived with his wife Maria (Dasha Blahova) and their two sons Shane and Danny. Peter O'Brien, who to this day is a very dear friend of mine, starred as Shane, and David Clencie, who I had worked with in an Australian miniseries called *I Can Jump Puddles*, was Danny, the character I had originally been cast as. Other residents of the street included Des Clarke and his wife Daphne (Paul Keane and Elaine Smith), and his somewhat interfering mother Eileen (Myra de Groot). And then there was Max's fiery sister Madge (Anne Charleston), whose legendary feuds on the street seemed to be anything but neighbourly.

My character, Scott, was the second son in the Robinson household. His father Jim, played by Alan Dale, who now stars in the American hit *Ugly Betty*, had been widowed, and so we lived with my 'Gran', who was brought to life by the actress Anne Haddy. When I first read the script I couldn't help but notice the parallels between Scott's life and my own, the only difference being that he had siblings.

There was his older, slightly Machiavellian brother Paul, played by Stefan Dennis (who, after a twelve-year absence from the show, has since reprised his role), his sister Julie (the actress Vikki Blanche), and then there was Lucy, the youngest member of the family. I would like to put a name to her character but it would take too long, for over the years so many actresses played this part that Alan and I used to joke that the producers should have installed a revolving door at the front of our house. Of course, this was not unusual, for in the world of soap opera no actor is indispensable; what matters to the show is the character itself. Cast members can be dropped and replaced at a moment's notice. Indeed, my own character had originally been played by an actor called Darius Perkins, and despite the fact that we bore no resemblance to one another, none of my 'family' or 'friends' seemed to notice when I turned up as the new Scott.

When Channel Ten decided to take on *Neighbours* there was no question that it was something of a gamble for them. Although the series had been well-received by the critics when it was on Channel Seven, the ratings hadn't been good. It had fared reasonably well in its home territory of Victoria, but it hadn't gained a good following outside of that, and it had completely underperformed in the crucial Sydney market. It could be argued that the reason for this was simply that Channel Seven hadn't given it a prime-time billing: in Sydney it was shown at five thirty in the afternoon, whereas in Melbourne and the other regions it was aired at six thirty. Had it been moved into the prime-time peak slot on Channel Seven, the chances were the network would have picked up a larger audience, but the executives were not prepared to do that.

Channel Ten quickly recognised the mistakes that Channel Seven had made and knew that if the soap was going to be a hit they were not only going to have to give it the push it so desperately needed but they would have to revamp the show so that it appealed to a wider audience. As soon as they acquired the soap they allocated it the much-coveted prime-time 7 p.m. slot, for this was the time in the evening when families across Australia sat down to watch television together. But the suits at the network knew that this wasn't enough – if they were going to get serious ratings it was crucial for them to capture a younger market, and if they were to do that then the show was going to have to become more youthful in its appeal.

As a family-based soap there had always been children and teenagers in *Neighbours*, but the real drama in the soap had never really included them, revolving instead around the ups and downs of the older characters in the street. Much to the chagrin of some of the older cast members on the soap, Channel Ten knew this was going to have to change, and at once they instructed their scriptwriters to develop the characters of the younger members of the cast and start writing storylines for them as well. The children and teenagers were no longer incidental to the main storylines but from then on would be integral to them.

It would be fair to say that there was a lot of tension on set when we first started working with the new scripts. Many of the older actors believed they were being sidelined, replaced instead by a bunch of kids who didn't know what they were doing, and so they treated the younger cast with a certain amount of hostility – if they made a mistake, missed a cue or fluffed up a line they would really get it in the neck. Luckily for me I was never in their line of fire; I guess they assumed that by carrying the Donovan name I had some kind of pedigree.

Only too aware of just how fragile actors' egos can be, the production company did their best to try to appease the situation, and there were a lot of meetings behind closed doors back then. But they also knew that if *Neighbours* was to succeed it had to become more youth-orientated. The original characters of Shane, Danny, Scott and Lucy were developed, and in the next few months they would introduce new ones too. There was Annie Jones, who played plain Jane Harris; Craig McLachlan, who was cast as Madge's son Henry; and, although it is almost hard to believe now, given his Hollywood success, there was also Guy Pearce (Pearcy), who played Jane's boyfriend Mike Young.

To keep continuity going as the programme moved networks, the producers knew that for the moment they would have to hold on to the original cast, but they were quite prepared to drop characters that they felt didn't quite work. One week these actors would be on set, acting out

their scenes, and the next they'd be clearing their belong-
ings out of the trailer, having been deftly written out, their
characters confined to soap history and kept alive only by a
passing line in the script when the plot required it. Characters were forever going to Queensland, never to return.
And if the production company felt for a moment that any
of the cast were getting slightly too big for their boots then
they would quickly be brought into line. The threat of
being sent to 'Brisbane' was enough to get any of us under
control.

I adapted to life on the soap quickly. I got on with many
of the younger cast members and made it my business to get
to know the older ones too. It's a funny thing working on a
soap, because after a while your off-screen relationships can
quite unintentionally start to mirror your on-screen ones.
The actors who played Scott's friends Jane, Mike, Shane
and Danny became my friends, and when we weren't on set
working we spent a lot of time together messing about
behind the scenes. Anne Haddy became something of a
surrogate grandmother to me, and Alan Dale and I became
extremely close off-camera as well as on screen. I learned a
great deal from him during my time on the show.

Given the hours we were working it probably wasn't
surprising that we eventually all became as close as we did.
Neighbours was aired five times a week, in 22-minute
episodes, for 49 weeks of the year, and so we kept long
hours. If we weren't at the studios in Nunawading shooting
the internal scenes then we were on location at Pin Oak

Court, in nearby Vermont Street, which was used to represent the exterior of Ramsay Street. It was an actual street, with actual residents, and although I know they were paid pretty generously for the loan of their cul-de-sac I'm not sure how they put up with us. On location days the trailers would park in the neighbouring street and cast and crew would descend on their otherwise sleepy little close. On each day of filming the residents would have to move their cars from their driveways to make way for the characters' ones. They would have actors outside their front doorways pretending to come and go, and some dotted round their gardens talking to each other over hedges. They would have soundmen in their driveways, and cameras and lights pointing at their properties. Outside on the forecourt on any given day there would be a fight, an accident, a cricket match, a party, or a game of football. It must have been a living hell, but somehow they coped and today Pin Oak Court is a tourist attraction – in fact it is the highlight of the Official *Neighbours* Tour, and every day crowds of people arrive in buses to come and get their little fix of television history. You can even visit a replica set of the Robinsons' house at the Melbourne Museum.

After four or five weeks of filming we were given a month off for our Christmas break. Dad and Marlene had taken a flat in Rose Bay, in Sydney, which was right on the waterfront, and we spent Christmas and New Year there as a family with Paul, who was now four years old. I remember that break like it was yesterday because I had never felt so free or independent in my life. I had just learned that I had passed my HSC, gaining good marks in politics, economics and accountancy. As respectable as my grades were, I have to be honest – they weren't exactly going to take me into the hallowed halls of Oxford, Harvard, or even Melbourne University, but that didn't matter to me, for uni had never been an option. All that counted was that I had passed, and in any case I didn't need to further my education now for I had a job, something that had only really hit home when I'd received and cashed my first paycheque from Grundy's earlier that month.

The first episode of the revamped *Neighbours* was to be aired on 20 January 1986. It had been heavily advertised in the press, and fans and critics alike were eagerly awaiting its new incarnation. But this alone was not enough for Channel Ten. They knew that with its new prime-time slot the show would get a respectable audience in and around Melbourne, but they were also well aware that if the programme was to become a national success, and not just a regional one, then they had to crack Sydney, and so they turned to their Director of Publicity, Brian Walsh, and put him on the project.

Brian is very much a man with two sides to his character. When he is off-duty you couldn't want for better company, because he is extremely friendly, sharp-witted and pretty easy-going, but catch him in business mode and he is like a formidable force of nature who won't let anything or anyone stand in his way. When it comes to marketing a product he is almost Napoleonic in his strategy, and that's how he was when he was given the task of putting *Neighbours* on the map. From the outset he regarded *Neighbours* not as a show, but as a brand. Brian had started his career in radio but it wasn't until he went into television that he really found his calling, for he was absolutely passionate about TV.

In the run-up to 20 January, Brian was determined to get the soap and its cast into public consciousness and set upon a marketing blitz that had never been seen in Australia before. There were radio and television interviews, press days, personal appearances, photo shoots with newspapers and magazines – it was a complete media onslaught. The public, whether they liked it or not, would know exactly who we were by the time we hit their screens. He'd done a good job, for there was no escaping us, but that wasn't enough for him. He knew he still had to get Sydney on board, so that January he arranged for all the cast members, old and new, to travel there for a final personal appearance: the *Neighbours* launch party. He flew the entire cast out from Melbourne, put us up in one of the city's best hotels, and the following day he threw a party on a luxury yacht and invited all the press to come and join us as we cruised around the harbour. If that didn't generate interest in the show, he figured, nothing would.

For some reason I was running a little late on the afternoon of the launch and was slightly out of breath as I boarded the boat. I had never met Brian before and this wasn't the greatest of starts. When we were introduced he looked me up and down as he carried on talking into his mobile telephone, which was the size of a brick. I remember that moment as though it were yesterday. I was standing there in my skate shorts and my souvenir Sydney Theatre T-shirt, which had been given to me when Dad had played *Chicago* there, my hair flying everywhere. Although Brian was known for his charm, I had also heard how driven he was when it came to business, and I was terrified that he was going to have a go at me for not being professional, but instead he just flashed me one of his trademark grins.

'I'm Jason ...' I said, trying to get my breath back.

'I know exactly who you are,' he replied. 'That's my job.'

The rest of the cast had already gathered on the deck and were starting to line up for the photographers, so I went over to join them and took my place. Suddenly, Judy, a publicist from Channel Ten's Sydney office, came over and tried to shoo me out of the way.

'No, not you ... move out the way. It's a cast photograph.'

I could feel my cheeks starting to burn when a voice called out from behind the press pack.

'*Hello! Excuse me! Are you there?*' Brian screeched at Judy. He pushed his way through the photographers, grabbed my arm and put me back in the line-up. 'You do know who *this* is, don't you, Judy?' he tutted theatrically.

As the boat slowly made its way out of its mooring I realised that I had run out of cigarettes. I began rummaging around in my bag, patting down my pockets to see if I had overlooked them.

'What's wrong?' Brian asked.

'It's nothing. I just forgot my ciggies, that's all.'

'Don't worry, we'll get you some.'

'Have you got some spares on board?'

'I doubt it. But don't worry, we'll stop at the next port and someone can go and get you some.'

And, to my amazement, that's exactly what happened. The boat docked at the next port and a member of the crew was instructed to go and buy me not just a packet but a carton of cigarettes. I didn't even have to pay for them. 'Put them on the card!' shouted Brian as the boy stepped off the boat. 'The *company* card!'

It was the strangest thing, but as I lit up I couldn't help feeling that this was it: this was going to be really big, and I was actually part of it. I'd already had the experience of working in TV, but I had never known anything like this: fancy hotels, parties on yachts, corporate entertainment and hospitality, it was like a whole new world to me. I had just got my first taste of what it was like to be a star.

I was nervous watching that first episode of *Neighbours*, but, as the credits rolled at the end of the show and that murderously catchy Tony Hatch song started to play again, I have to say I came away thinking that it wasn't that bad. I certainly wasn't Laurence Olivier, but then the part didn't require Laurence Olivier. It needed a blond, blue-eyed, slightly tanned, happy-go-lucky kid who typified a generation of Australian teenagers.

I settled into life on set well. The hours could be long but I wasn't averse to a bit of hard work, and as Dad kept pointing out to me there were far worse jobs I could be doing. 'Make the most of it,' he said, and I did. I made friends with the cast and crew and tried to learn from them all. When I was in-between takes I would hang out in the green room and practise my guitar or I'd fly through the corridors of the studio on my skateboard.

Although I wasn't taking home mega-bucks I was earning a hell of a lot more money than most kids of my age. Dad was adamant that I put most of it away and invest it for the future. 'You never know what's going to happen in this game,' he would say to me. And so, as the cheques came in, I would take them down to the local State Bank branch and deposit them into my savings account – like father, like son. I didn't need much money at the time as it was. I was still living at home so I had no overheads, and Grundy's were pretty generous when it came to expenses. All the cast members were allocated chequebooks full of cab charges to take us to and from the set, and when we were working on location we ate and drank for free. And, in any case, I didn't have that much opportunity to spend the money I was earning. What free time I did have was always spent with James down at the beach or back at one of our houses pulling bongs. The last thing I wanted to do on a day off was to go shopping. I just wasn't that type of kid.

In my first few weeks on set I took work very seriously. I was so conscious of not making a mistake or forgetting my lines that I'd spend hours before I went to bed at night going over my script for the following day. It was trial enough trying to get through a scene saying your lines and not falling over the set or the props, which were pretty bloody wobbly in those days. But as time went on I began to get more confident and it started to come more easily to me. 'Never take things in your stride,' Dad was always telling me. 'You can't afford to become complacent as an actor, you must always keep on your toes. Listen carefully and observe everything.'

I guess I should have listened to him, but three months into filming I was becoming a little more relaxed about work. On one afternoon, when I had finished all my scenes for the day, David Clencie asked me whether I wanted to share a joint with him.

I'd never smoked at work before but this was all too tempting. I'd done all my work for the day, after all. So David and I snuck round the back of the set of 'Lassiter's Hotel', a glorified motel that Channel Ten had written into the show to give it a touch of 'glamour'. We were sitting on the ground, smoking, laughing, and getting progressively more stoned, when I suddenly heard my name called.

'Jason! Jason! Has anyone seen Jason?' It was the assistant director.

'No, why?' someone shouted back.

'We need him back on set. We've had to change the shooting schedule and we need him now.'

'Fucking hell!' I spluttered.

'Mate, what are you going to do?' said David, trying to suppress his laughter.

'I guess I'll have to go. I haven't got much choice, have I?'

And so, having stubbed out my doobie, cleaned my teeth in the make-up room, put eye drops into my eyes and dusted myself down, I went back onto the set. I tried to act as normally as possible but it was an absolute disaster. My head was a complete fog, my mouth was dry, my eyes were so pinned they looked like piss-holes in the snow, I couldn't remember any of my lines and I kept banging into people.

After that I made a decision – never, ever mix drugs with work again.

Now that I had got into the swing of things at work and had got to grips with the character, I decided that I wanted to develop him in some way because I was conscious of the fact that he was slightly two-dimensional. I had the look, I had the lines, but I felt that it wasn't enough. I wanted to bring him to life. As I knew that I had primarily been cast for the role because I fitted the bill in some way, I decided that this was my best starting point. I would make Scott an extension of myself. There was no point in just standing still and saying my lines because I knew that wasn't convincing.

Scott was a teenage boy full of energy and enthusiasm for everything. He had to be running around, always on the move. I knew from the way I was that Scott wouldn't just walk through a door when he entered a room, he had to burst through it. He couldn't sit at a table with his hands by his sides, he'd be playing with something, fidgeting with a piece of fruit from the bowl, fiddling with his clothes, messing up his hair. Sid, one of the cameramen I worked with at the time, enjoyed what I was doing and encouraged me to take it further, and so I started to think when I looked at a scene – How would *I* react to that? What would *I* do if that was me? I asked the costume people whether we could work on Scott's clothes. There was nothing wrong with what they had put him in – a selection of shorts and T-shirts – but I knew that if we wanted Scott to be as true to life as possible we had to get it just right. We had to get him dressing like the other boys I knew in Melbourne at the time. T-shirts had to be long, surf shorts had to stop at the calf. And the other thing Scott needed, if he was to be the archetypal Australian kid, was a skateboard. The producers loved the idea, and not only gave me a board but let me ride it in the opening credits. Within four months I had the character exactly where I wanted him to be.

There is no question that in its new incarnation *Neighbours* was a lot more popular than it had ever been on Channel Seven, and, thanks to a strong cast, the new sense of energy the producers had injected into the show, and Brian's publicity work, we had begun to get a following in

Sydney. But for Channel Ten this wasn't enough: they knew there was room for improvement, and in the spring of that year they decided to introduce some new blood into the show.

I had no idea who was coming on board, for the actors were always the last to know. All we'd been told was that in the next few weeks there would be a couple of new additions to the cast. Word had it that Madge was gaining a daughter – but no one thought very much about it, since another great tradition in soaps is for characters to suddenly discover, quite out of the blue, that they have a long-lost child.

I was sitting in the costume trailer one morning having my make-up done when I felt a tap on my shoulder. 'Jason ...'

I turned round and I must have looked blankly at her, judging by the next thing she said to me.

'You do remember me, don't you?'

'Er ...'

'You and me, running around an airport ... *Skyways* ...'

'Kylie?'

Chapter Six

Kylie said to Jason ...

SHE HAD BEEN on set for less than a week when she hit me. And as slight and petite as she is, let me tell you, Kylie certainly knows how to throw a mean punch. She had quite a swing on her and a good aim too, for her fist met the right side of my jaw with a good clean blow. Of course, I knew I had it coming to me, I'd been prepared for it for days. It was in the script, after all – the dramatic climax to our very first scene together.

Scott had been walking home from a trip to the 'coffee shop' when he spotted an intruder trying to climb through the window of No. 22 Ramsay Street. Always keen to save the day, Scott ran down the street in an attempt to stop them, only to be rewarded with a blow to the face for his efforts. When he realised that the intruder was not actually a petty criminal after all, but none other than his childhood friend Charlene Mitchell, whom he hadn't seen for years, he was stunned. Cue a credit roll.

'Please don't tell me we have to do that again!' I moaned, clutching my chin, as the director called cut.

'No, you're fine – both of you. It was just great, really great, well done.'

The character of Charlene, or 'Lenny' as she was known, was introduced into the soap in the first half of 1986. She had arrived in Ramsay Street on the back of a truck, hitch-hiking her way into the drama, from a place called Coffs Harbour. According to her back story, which would have been raced through by the writers, for they never liked to get too bogged down with minutiae like that, she had got bored of living with her father and wanted a fresh start in Erinsborough with her mother, Madge. Charlene was quite a wild kid, a tomboy with a fiery temperament and a will of steel. She answered to no one but herself, much to her mother's exasperation.

Our casting agent Jan Russ had been keen to get Kylie into the soap from the beginning. She had seen her in *The Henderson Kids* and *The Sullivans* and knew that she would work well in the soap, but it had been a question of timing. Like me, Kylie hadn't been available for work when *Neighbours* began on Channel Seven, and when the soap restarted in January the writers needed time to formulate a character that would be right for her to play. Once they had it, from her very first episodes on the soap Charlene gained a huge following and it was easy to see why. Kylie, by her own admission, was not the greatest actor back then – none of us were – and yet there was something so fresh and beguiling about her, and it was clear from watching the rushes of her first scenes on the soap that the camera absolutely loved her.

I could be forgiven for not recognising Kylie when she had reintroduced herself in the costume trailer that morning. The last time we had seen each other we had been nothing more than kids, and we had both done a lot of growing up in those intervening years. The little girl I had met on the set of *Skyways* had become a teenager. She may have been petite but she had a good figure, big blue eyes and a bobble of fair curly hair that fell over her shoulders. She looked like a little doll.

And yet, as pretty as she was, I wasn't attracted to Kylie at first, but I liked her a lot and it wasn't long before we became friends. As we got to know each other more it became clear that we had a lot in common. Kylie lived not far from me in a place called Surrey Hills and we moved in similar circles. In her spare time Kylie used to hang out with her friends at the Harold Holt Memorial Pool, in Malvern, a complex of indoor and outdoor pools with a huge diving tower. It was my local pool and it was where Dad had first taught me to swim. It was named after the former Australian prime minister, which when you think about it is a rather unfortunate tribute, given the fact that poor Mr Holt is supposed to have died drowning off the Portsea coast within his first year of office. But of course, all that had very little bearing on the kids who congregated at the pool at the weekends and during the holidays. The boys would pedal up there on their pushbikes, in their faded jeans and white T-shirts, one sleeve folded over at the top so as to keep their packet of Winfield Reds in place, even though they could just as easily have stored them in their trouser pockets. And as they drew up to the complex the girls would start to arrive in groups, heading to changing rooms to get into their cossies, and they would all spend the rest of the day hanging out there, eyeing one another up. As a surfer I didn't do the Harold Holt, for I was more of a beach boy. But, coming from Malvern, I knew a lot of the people who went there, so we had mutual friends – Blackie, Stace and Fletch, to name a few.

And then there was the fact that Kylie and I had similar childhoods, insofar as we had both done a lot of television work. Although Kylie's parents weren't in the entertainment industry, her father, Ron, was an accountant, and while her mother Carol's sole focus was raising her three children, she came from a theatrical background. Kylie's aunt, Sue Jones, was and still is a respected actress in Australia, and so Sue and my father knew a lot of the same people.

Kylie's younger sister Dannii was also in the business. Before she found fame in *Home and Away*, Dannii was a singer, and when I first met her she had been on a children's variety show called *Young Talent Time*. At that stage Dannii was far better known than Kylie – in fact, it would be fair to say that she was one of the most famous kids on Australian television.

In real life Kylie was very different from her alter ego. Although Charlene was a deeply lovable character she was also brash and impulsive, prone to acting before she thought. She seemed to be constantly getting herself into scrapes, staying out late at night, going off drinking, or winding her mother up.

Kylie, on the other hand, was a sensitive soul. She was deeply contemplative and in many ways quite reserved. When she wasn't filming you would find her sitting quietly in the corner of the studio on her own, going over her scripts or happily weaving a basket or working on her needlepoint, for she was very into her crafts. She didn't like late nights, she never drank, and she would certainly never have deliberately gone out to upset her parents, for they were everything to her. And in many ways it was this relationship that really defined her. For someone who had achieved so much so young, she was extremely grounded. Ron and Carol had always encouraged their children to follow their dreams, but made sure that their feet remained firmly fixed on the ground. At work, Dannii and Kylie may have been stars, but when they returned to the family home in the evening they were treated like normal kids. As a result, Kylie didn't take anything or anyone for granted, and this made her very easy to work with. Even when she was at the height of her fame at the end of that decade she never let it go to her head. She never had any airs and graces, there was nothing of the diva about her; she was just a very normal, good-natured girl. But one of the qualities I admired most in Kylie then was her strength of character. She approached everything she did with such a sense of steely determination and focus that looking back now it hardly surprises me that she has gone on to achieve all that she has.

It helped that Kylie and I got on well because, long before we even shot that first scene together and the director picked up on the obvious spark between us, the producers had decided that our characters would become involved with one another. When I saw the scripts I was quite relieved for Scott, as all he ever seemed to do was skate in and out of scenes doing his paper round, or spend hours sitting round the kitchen table talking to Jim and Helen, or hang out with Mike in the coffee shop, which was all very well and good but I couldn't help feeling that he could be doing something else. In the soap, Scott was seventeen years old and was supposed to be a red-blooded young man. Everyone except me seemed to be paired off. Even Mike had a girlfriend – even if he didn't like her very much. Surely it was about time Scott found romance?

I doubt very much that when the scriptwriters started to pen our first scenes together they ever envisaged for a moment that the relationship between Scott and Charlene would last as long as it did. And I know for a fact they didn't see our characters eventually walking up the aisle together. What they had on paper was the classic boy-and-girl-next-door relationship. Maybe, if they were lucky, they could string it out for six months or so, until it became stale and the audience got bored, and then they would move us on, for the key to success is to always keep the momentum going. Twists and turns, trysts and triangles, the daily cliff-hanger – these have always been essential components to a really good soap.

Right from the beginning it was clear to everyone that the relationship between the two characters worked. For starters, it had been a very good piece of casting, because we looked right together. It was a good physical match and I think people out there actually believed that we could be a couple. Secondly, we were lucky in that we had a good storyline. Scott and Charlene were Ramsay Street's very own Romeo and Juliet. We were two young lovers coming from families at war with one another – the Robinsons were the Montagues, and the Ramsays the Capulets. When our characters announced that we wanted to live together, both families were so opposed to the decision that they did every-thing they could to prevent it from happening. But, of course, this was soap, and unlike Shakespeare's romantic tragedy we were eventually allowed to have our happy ending.

But there was another reason why our pairing worked, and that was because there was a genuine on-screen chem-istry between us. There is no question that the rapport we had behind the scenes translated onto the small screen. In fact, the undercurrent between us was so strong that people we knew who watched the show kept asking whether there was something going on between us.

By Easter 1986, *Neighbours* had a reasonably good following. The ratings for the show were growing steadily and we were getting a lot of press coverage. Both Grundy's and Channel Ten were pleased with the way things were going, but, of course, this wasn't enough for Brian, he always had to go that extra mile. He didn't want *Neighbours* to be *one* of the most popular shows in Australia; it had to be up there at the top of the list, that was his priority. And it was at this time that Brian hit upon his most cunning plan to date: a 'personal appearances' tour of Australia, his rationale being that if the public wouldn't come to us, he would take us to them. Therefore, over the next few months the younger members of the cast travelled the length and breadth of the country doing a succession of meet-and-greet appearances. 'We have to create a buzz around the show, get everyone into a frenzy, cause a stir. You know what I'm saying?' Brian explained. And so he sent us out to shopping malls, parks and theatres to meet our fans, and hopefully to pick up some new ones along the way. We would make guest appearances at local fairs, where we would have our own stand. We would sign autographs, hand out goody bags full of *Neighbours* merchandise and meet our fans.

The culmination of this tour was an appearance at the Sydney Royal Easter Show. No Easter in Australia was ever complete without a trip to your local agricultural fair, and when I was young Gran had taken me to the one in

Melbourne as a treat. But this year it was different: instead of being with Gran, with her picnics of chicken sandwiches and tea, and heading off to the central ring to watch the cow parade, I was in Sydney with Brian, promoting *Neighbours* from our stand, as if we were his very own prized bulls, put on display for the crowds to admire.

When Brian first ran the idea past us I have to admit that I was unsure whether it would work. I had done a reasonable amount of personal appearances before. We'd get invited to turn up at events and clubs around Melbourne and would be paid handsomely for our time. Sometimes, on a good night, Peter O'Brien, Stefan Dennis and I could get two to three thousand Australian dollars each simply for showing up at a gig, which was a considerable amount of money in those days – but we had never done it in an official capacity, to promote the show. We were simply earning some extra cash on the side. Whenever we went to one of these gigs, I couldn't help but wonder whether anyone would bother to turn up. We weren't rock stars, after all; we were just a group of kids who worked on a soap. Why would anyone want to go out of their way to come and meet us? But, to my amazement, they came in their thousands. I remember standing in a shopping mall one day and literally being mobbed by all these teenagers, and when we turned up at the Sydney Show our presence there created such a frenzy that we couldn't even get back into the limo to get out. Instead, we had to be taken out of the arena in a paddy wagon.

For some reason the public couldn't get enough of us – or, to put it more accurately, of our characters. 'Mike! Scott! Charlene! Jane!' they would shout. It was all quite surreal – for we were never Guy, Jason, Kylie or Annie. Fans would come up to us and ask the most bizarre questions. 'Hey, Mike, where's Bouncer?' 'Where are Des and Daphne?' And when it came to me it was always about Charlene. 'What's going on with you two?' 'Why were you so mean to her last week?' 'Are you two going to marry one day?' It was as though they had no concept of what was real and what wasn't.

'Er … *Hello? Are you there?*' Brian said when I put this to him. 'Jason, when are you going to understand this game? This isn't about you, it's about your characters! That's what keeps them interested. Just let them believe what they want to. Keep them all guessing.'

And he was right – it wasn't about us, it was all about who we were on the soap. Our fans didn't care what *we* were getting up to in real life – all they cared about was our characters. It got to the point where we all learned to accept it and laugh about it. To this day it is something of a running joke between Guy Pearce and me. From time to time when I'm writing to him I will start my emails with the words, 'Dear Mike'. And he in turn writes back to Scott and, true to character, is always polite enough to ask after Charlene and enquire about our life in Brisbane, which always amuses me.

Although they could be hard work I quite liked these excursions and trips away. It was fun getting out of the studio for a while and being able to let our hair down and just be ourselves. Being on the road brought us all closer together and we formed some very genuine friendships with one another – and none more so than the one I shared with Kylie.

'I just don't know why you two don't get together,' Alan said to me one day. It was nearing the end of the year and we were getting ready for a scene together.

'Me and Kylie?'

'Yes, you and Kylie! Who else did you think I was talking about?'

'We're just friends, that's all. I don't find her attractive in that way ...'

'So you keep saying, but I don't believe you. You spend all your time together, you get on really well, and you are both single. So what's stopping you?'

I wasn't sure what to say. Like most teenage boys, my taste in girls was hardly very refined, and Kylie seemed to be the antithesis of the sort of busty Big M girl from the TV adverts that my friends and I used to lust over. She didn't dress provocatively, she hardly ever wore make-up; she didn't even sunbathe. She would turn up for work in the morning in her little tracksuit, her hair still wet from the shower, script in one hand and her packed lunch of rice cakes and homemade hummus in the other, like she didn't have a care in the world.

'Come on, Jason, just look at her! She is absolutely gorgeous.'

Now, as much as Alan was always the perfect gentleman, he loved women, and I couldn't help but think that had he been a) single, and b) twenty years younger that he might have liked to have had a crack at Kylie himself. But that aside, there was no denying that he was right. Kylie was gorgeous. She had always been a good-looking girl, but in recent months she had blossomed into something else. It was as though she had grown into herself, acquired a new sense of confidence. There was something different about her.

If I was to put a time onto Kylie's metamorphosis then it would be around the time that Charlene had dropped out of school, stopped wearing that daggy uniform, started her apprenticeship as a mechanic and stepped into those now infamous overalls.

'I don't think she sees me that way,' I told Alan.

'Are you kidding? She's mad about you, anyone can see that.'

Now, I'd had a couple of girlfriends in my time. I'd enjoyed a brief interlude with a really spunky girl called Caroline, but, if I am entirely honest about it, it was rather one-sided. Caroline had that sun-kissed look – blonde hair, light tan, freckles – and I was completely infatuated with her. We'd dated for a while, but after a couple of weeks it became quite apparent that she wasn't that interested in me. Next on the list was the lovely Kelly, and that had all been going swimmingly until Marlene caught us one afternoon in a rather compromising position, which kind of put paid to that relationship, as Kelly was far too embarrassed to ever set foot in the Donovan house again. And then there was Fleur – gorgeous in every way. The only thing that went against Fleur was her height: she was built like an Amazonian and, at six foot, she towered over me. I seemed to spend most of our time together trying to negotiate how to kiss her, and so eventually it died a natural death.

As lovely as all these girls were, I couldn't pretend for a moment that any of these relationships had been serious. They were just teenage romances that came and went within the blink of an eye.

I'd never been the type of boy to set my cap at someone. I guess that I was just too shy. I may have had a recognisable face and been relatively well-known, but that really didn't mean very much to me, because on the inside I was just as insecure as the next person – and, like any teenage boy, I was terrified of rejection. For me, relationships – the ones that have mattered to me – have always had to develop at their own pace. I could only get involved with someone and make that first move if I knew that they felt the same way.

I thought about what Alan had said over the next couple of weeks. Kylie was lovely; she was beautiful, sassy and a lot of fun to be around. There was no denying the fact that we got on well. We spent twelve hours a day on set together, which for most people would be enough as it was, but for some reason we still felt compelled to see each other when we weren't at work. We hung out together at weekends. She'd come out at night with James and me, we would go to movies and parties together, and spend afternoons whiling away time on the beach.

It never really comes as any surprise to me now when I hear stories about actors falling for one another on set, for the whole process is so incredibly intense that it is hard not to get caught up in the whirlwind, and I think that is what had started to happen to us.

There was a mental connection between us, the shared experience of working together day in and day out for the best part of a year, and, of course, there was the physical aspect of it too. Playing lovers on a television show is not like working side by side in an office environment, for it is part of your job to become intimate with one another. When you first start working together you follow the stage directions to the letter – the hand-holding, the hugs, the occasional kiss are all done on command – but once you realise there is a spark between you, these physical displays of intimacy blur into the moments when you are off-screen. And, as time went on, I realised that this was happening between us. The on-screen kiss between Scott and Charlene became a little more lingering; we'd add a hug that wasn't in the script into a scene; or our hands would brush against one another when the director had called cut. Sometimes I'd get her by the back of her overalls and pull her towards me. As they say in the business, there was a lot of business going on between us.

Towards the end of the year the producers sent the characters of Scott and Charlene and Mike and Jane to Sydney.

Channel Ten were now so keen to crack the all-important Sydney market that they thought it would be a good idea to start using it as a location in the soap, so the four of us packed our bags and flew there for a week of filming.

I have little recollection of why we were supposed to be there in terms of the storyline, for I remember that trip for other reasons. Because it was there, in the rather less-than-romantic surroundings of the Sydney Travelodge, that Kylie and I admitted our feelings for one another and finally got together.

Chapter Seven

Invisible Touch

WHEN WORD GOT round the set that Kylie and I were now together I don't think anyone was surprised. They had seen it coming a mile off and the general consensus was, 'What took you so long?' Everyone seemed to be happy for us. Alan in particular couldn't contain his glee. Not only was he thrilled for us, but I think he was rather chuffed with his little piece of matchmaking. Both Dad and Marlene were pleased when I told them I was seeing Kylie. They had liked her from the moment I brought her home for the first time, and I guess, like most people we were close to, they'd realised it was just a question of time before we admitted our feelings for one another.

As much as Dad and Marlene loved Kylie, because she was so close to her parents we seemed to spend much more of our time at the Minogues' house than we did at Union Street during the initial stages of our relationship, but that never bothered me because I loved being there. Even though Ron and Carol had obviously done well for themselves there was nothing grand about their house in Surrey Hills. If anything it was quite modest, but what made their home so special was the atmosphere there: it was always full of a lot of laughter and love. By anyone's standards the Minogues were a model family – but to me, coming from the background I did, they were so much more than that. They were the type of family I used to dream of belonging to when I was a small boy. Ron, who adored his three children, had got the whole father act completely spot on. He was involved in their lives but never interfered; he was protective of them all without being overbearing. Carol was kind, gentle and loving; she was the type of woman you could imagine telling anything to, and she was extremely selfless. On top of all this they were happily married, and you could tell that they were still deeply in love with one another.

Kylie, Dannii and their brother Brendan were all close. Despite working in the same industry, contrary to what many people thought at the time and still try to assert to this day, there was no deep rivalry between Kylie and Dannii. There was a healthy competitive spirit between them, which was only natural given that they were sisters and so close in age, but they were never at each other's throats. At the end of the day they were sisters and they loved each other, and as it was they were very different people. Dannii was, without a doubt, the more outrageous of the two, she had something of a wild streak about her, while Kylie was more like her mother and was much more contained. What was great about Ron and Carol was that they never set their children off against each other, they simply encouraged them to get on with life at their own pace and supported them in anything they did.

All the kids were encouraged to bring their friends home, and there was something of an open-door policy in their house. If you pitched up just as they were sitting down together for lunch or dinner, you were encouraged, if not forced by Carol, into joining them. The more the merrier was her attitude, and there was always plenty to go round. When I started seeing Kylie, the Minogues welcomed me into their home and treated me as though I was a member of their family, which really touched me. I was even allowed to spend the night in Kylie's room – on Ron and Carol's proviso that I didn't share their daughter's bed, of course.

Kylie was my first proper girlfriend and my first real love affair, and as such those initial few months together were intoxicating. I had never felt this way about anyone, it was all so new, so exciting, and I don't think that I had ever felt so happy. In those first months together I think we both felt like we were walking on air and we hated being apart from one another. It wasn't enough that we spent twelve hours a day together at the studio, we wanted to spend every waking hour together. We were inseparable.

Even though we were working in such a public industry, and we were both relatively well-known and earned much more than any of our contemporaries, I would say that ours was a very normal teenage relationship. At weekends we would go swimming in the morning or head down to South Melbourne to have floatation tank sessions, which was a bit of a trend back then. We would hang out on the Toorak Road or Chapel Street, and browse round the clothes and record shops. In the evening, if we weren't going to the movies we would have dinner at the local Italian or Japanese restaurants and order rounds of garlic bread, salads, chicken kievs, calamari and tempura because those were our favourite foods. If we were with our friends then we would go to the beach, eat pizza or while away the afternoons in cafes. Kylie and I had just got into cappuccinos at around that time, and she was simply mad about them. She didn't like them to be too strong, and they had to have a lot of frothy milk on the top.

Kylie didn't drink alcohol, she didn't smoke, and she certainly didn't experiment with drugs. She was social and had a close-knit group of girlfriends but she wasn't what I would call a party girl. Sure, she liked to go out and loved to dance, but she would never stay out late. She was very into fashion and liked to design and make her clothes. When I asked her one day why she didn't just buy some designer outfits – she could afford them, after all, or could have got them for free given her profile – she looked rather taken aback. 'But that would take all the fun out of it,' she explained. She was a good seamstress, she enjoyed her needlepoint and lacework, and I sometimes think that if Kylie's career hadn't gone in the direction it did, she would have happily pursued work in the fashion industry.

Our other favourite pastime was to go on road trips together. I had applied for my driving permit on the very first day I was legally entitled to it and had passed my test just months later. As soon as I had that licence in my hand I bought myself a white Volkswagen Golf. It was the first big purchase I had made since starting on *Neighbours* and I really loved that car. Sure, I had enough money in the bank to buy something a little more flash, but the car suited me well, and in any case I had promised Dad that I wouldn't get myself a death trap. Kylie had the most beautiful old Morris, which she had bought out of her own money. Ron, who was a complete car fanatic, had done the negotiating and made the actual purchase after a thorough inspection. But she hadn't passed her test yet. I think that's the only time I have ever seen Kylie really frustrated by anything. She was the type of person who picked up things almost instinctively. She could learn a script, master a dance routine, make a song her own within just a couple of minutes, but when it came to that gear shift she just couldn't do it. 'Arghh!' she would scream when Ron and I would try to give her a lesson in the backstreets of Surrey Hills. 'Why can't I do this? What's wrong with me?' And so the driving always fell to me, but I didn't mind about that, there was nothing I liked more than sitting behind the wheel of my car. It made me feel so free, so independent.

We'd head off down the Great Ocean Road to Bells Beach, Lorne and Phillip Island. I had a box of cassettes in the car and Kylie would play DJ as I concentrated on the road. We

The early 1900s version of a people carrier – a 'DONO-Van' maybe?! My grandfather and grandmother are in the second seat from the front with my uncle on their lap.

My great grandfather George Arnsby standing outside his shop – the only licensed cow keepers in Kensington and Chelsea.

Left Me with my mother. I hadn't seen this photo before. Now I know where Zac gets his infectious grin.

Below I was about six years old here. Dad had to take me to work with him as there was a problem with babysitters and I didn't want to go. Hence the pissed-off look.

Above Dad was one of the leading cast members of the Australian television police drama series *Division 4* in the Seventies. I was snapped popping out of the makeup trailer.

Above My grandmother Joan. One of the real inspirations of my life. I miss her.

Above My father and me at my cousins the McArds' house in the Seventies. I remember that t-shirt very well. I must have been around five or six.

Left Ah, the national Australian symbol. Big rats, basically. I must have been around the age of five when I went for a day trip with Dad to Healesville Sanctuary, just outside Melbourne.

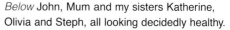

Below John, Mum and my sisters Katherine, Olivia and Steph, all looking decidedly healthy.

Above 25 October 1981.
At home in Union Street
on the day of my dad and
Marlene's wedding. I felt so
proud and honoured to be
best man, but at the tender
age of thirteen, I was
extremely nervous! As always,
Marlene looked gorgeous.

Right My brother Paul and
me outside our house on
Union Street, shortly after
I joined *Neighbours*.

Above The mullet at its best, resting on the shoulders of the man formerly known as Scott Robinson. In those days lack of hair was never a problem. I envy those bad hair days now!

Above Australia Post paying tribute to 50 years of Australian television. What an honour (for Scott and Charlene) to be recognized in this way.

Above On the set of 'Everyday' in London. The video was directed by Pete Cornish.

Above A classic publicity shot of Dad and me back in the *Neighbours* days. Thank God my mullet had gone by then.

Above At Rock Circus, next to my Madame Tussauds waxwork.

Left and below It's nice to feel that I was an integral part of music culture in the late Eighties. Love them or hate them, Stock, Aitken and Waterman had a massive impact on British music and sometimes it takes reflection (or history) to put things in perspective.

Far left Any opportunity to take off that shirt and show a bit of flesh. Love the pursed lips!

Left Smash Hits was *the* pop magazine of the Eighties.

Right The gang from *Neighbours*!

Below Carving it up in Hikkedwa, Sri Lanka. One of the great surfing trips of my life. Having just finished *Joseph*, I met James McGuire in Sri Lanka and we smoked pot, rode motorbikes and surfed for two weeks solid.

This shoot with Simon Fowler was specifically designed with the thought of my *Joseph* stint coming up. Simon shot me on many occasions and I always thought his lighting was superb.

had similar music tastes and liked to listen to The The, The Beatles, New Order, Midnight Oil, Kate Bush, Peter Gabriel, U2 and Heaven 17. One of our favourite's songs was 'You're the Voice' by John Farnham, which had been released that year on his *Whispering Jack* album. We would crank up the volume as far as it would go and sing along to it together at the tops of our voices, and once it came to an end we invariably ended up rewinding it and playing it all over again. But if I had to select a single piece of music to remind me of that era then it would have to be 'Invisible Touch' by Genesis. As far as I was concerned that song could have been Kylie's signature tune, and still to this day when I hear it played I am reminded of her.

We had been going out with each other for a couple of months when Kylie and I got a two-week break from *Neighbours*, and so we decided to take our first holiday together. We had been thinking about going to Queensland or maybe even taking a package trip to Hawaii, but Marlene, who, let's face it, had been a bit of a hippy chick in her time and had enjoyed travelling, encouraged us to spread our wings a little bit and be more adventurous. 'What about Bali?' she suggested one evening when we were still trying to figure out where to go.

'Bali?'

'Why not? It's one of the most beautiful places I've ever been to. Great weather, beautiful beaches, the people are gorgeous and it's very spiritual. I promise you, Jason, you would *love* it. Trust me!'

I looked at Kylie. 'What do you think?'

'Why not?'

'Bali it is then.'

Arriving at our hotel in Kuta on the first day of our holiday I thought that once again I had to hand it to Marlene. Bali was everything she'd said it would be, and to this day it is one of my favourite places on the entire planet. The island was beautiful, the climate was perfect, and the people couldn't have been friendlier. In the two weeks we were there we did the full-on Bali experience. We hired a VW Beetle – convertible, of course. We beach-hopped, went horse-riding, bought dodgy contraband cassettes, and had matching leather jackets made, which Kylie designed. We watched the sun come up on the beach in Nusa Dua, visited a monkey forest, where one of the little critters made off with one of Kylie's earrings, and – as much as I am really loath to admit to this detail – had our hair braided.

The other time-old tradition we followed as first-timers to the island was to come down with a very unpleasant bout of Bali belly. Poor Kylie got it so badly that there was a moment when we thought she might have to be hospitalised. She is hardly the biggest girl in the world as it is, but when she came back from that holiday she'd lost so much weight she'd have given all those LA size zeros a real run for their money.

That trip was a first for me in so many ways. It was the first time I had taken a holiday abroad on my own, which was daunting for a boy my age. The safety deposit box was my best friend. It was the first time that I had visited a country whose culture and language was different to that of my own. I remember walking down the beach one evening and seeing a couple of dead dogs lying there and being quite taken aback, for you just didn't see that kind of thing in Melbourne.

But, most significantly of all, it was the first time I'd spent more than a night alone with a girl. And even though we had our first proper fight on that trip – which was so heated we ended up walking off in different directions vowing never to speak to each other again (for the record I only managed three steps before running after her and begging for forgiveness) – it was on that holiday that I realised I was falling in love with Kylie.

It was an emotion that I had never experienced in my life before, one so intense that it swung like a heavy pendulum between feelings of absolute euphoria and complete and utter pain, with seemingly nothing in between. Whether she felt the same I cannot say, but for me this was the real deal. She was 'the one', as far as I was concerned: my first true love. I couldn't imagine ever feeling this way about anyone again. I couldn't see my life without her. I wanted to be with her forever.

When we got back from Bali I set about finalising the paperwork on a house I had just bought in Burnley, Rich-mond. Dad had been encouraging me for some time to invest in a property, and I decided to follow his advice. In the year I had been working on *Neighbours* I had made a considerable amount of money. Although we weren't paid an extortionate salary on the soap, we were getting around $350 an episode, and with the fixed guarantee of appearing in at least two a week, on average I was taking home $1000 a week, which back then was worth a lot more than it is today, plus any money that I earnt doing personal appearances. Of course, if your storyline was bigger, your wages would reflect that, so if you were in it all week you would be pocketing close to two thousand bucks, and if you added to this the fees we took home from our personal appearances, it amounted to quite a tidy sum. The fact was, after just a year in the soap I now had a deposit for my first home, which wasn't bad given the fact I had yet to celebrate my nineteenth birthday.

Dad was by no means throwing me out of Union Street. I knew that he was happy for me to stay on under his roof, but I felt it was time to go. I wanted my own place, I wanted some privacy, especially now I was in a serious relationship, and I was excited about being able to stand on my own two feet for the first time in my life.

On the advice of Dad and Ron I invested my capital in the suburb of Richmond, which at the time was slightly down-at-heel. I would hardly say it was a ghetto, but it wasn't one of the most desirable areas that Melbourne had to offer. Yet Dad and Ron knew that Richmond had a lot of investment potential and, as Melbourne spread out into the suburbs, they both realised that one day this area would become hot and I would see a good return for my money.

Dad had always had a nose for property, and I knew that Ron, as an accountant, had a good sense for these things too, and so I put down a deposit on my first place there. The house was on Gibdon Street in Burnley and it cost a cool $75,000, and, despite the fact that it was on one of the noisiest streets in the area and stood opposite a yeast factory, I reckoned it was worth every penny. In the months that followed, Ron started to invest in the area too on behalf of Kylie and Dannii, and I would go on to buy another property. Dad used to joke that if we carried on ploughing money into the area they would have to rename Richmond after us.

When I moved into the house later that year I initially rather hoped Kylie would join me, but it seemed she wasn't ready. Living at home gave her a sense of security and I don't think she was prepared to quite literally close that door once and for all, and, in any case, I know that Ron had his reservations. He was well aware of the fact that Kylie was of an age when she would soon fly the nest, and he was happy for us to live together, but as keen as he was for her to invest in Richmond he didn't really like the idea of her living there, for the street I lived on wasn't one of the safest. As it was, it was probably good that we didn't rush into things, for I soon discovered that I quite liked having my own space.

Kylie did come and stay, though, and at weekends we got quite into playing house. I loved my Saturday mornings there. We would get up early and head off to Prahran to stock up on food for the weekend. On Sundays we would go to Camberwell, to the mother of all second-hand markets, and search the stands for furniture and bric-a-brac with which to fill the house. With Kylie's help I decorated, painting my new place from top to bottom, and in the spare room we set up her sewing machine so she would have a space of her own to work in. My friend James was a constant visitor to the house, so much so that we reasoned pretty early on that it would be much simpler for everyone if he just moved in, and so he did.

At the very beginning of our relationship Kylie and I had made a conscious decision to keep it away from the press. It was early days for us and we were still getting to know one another and enjoying the time we had together. We wanted to keep our relationship private and hold something back for ourselves – our fans had the romance between Scott and Charlene to get on with after all, and we both realised that we had nothing to gain by going public with it.

The show's producers supported our decision. They understood what we were saying, but without being too cynical about it they also had their own agenda. If Kylie and I admitted to our relationship we could be in danger of alienating our teenage fan base. We needed to look as though we were available, that any one of our fans stood a chance with us, and so it suited them for us to keep quiet. If we were asked in an interview whether we were an item we followed Channel Ten's brief and, if I'm honest, our own intuition. 'We're just really good friends,' we would tell the press.

As amazing as it seems today, it wasn't that difficult to keep our relationship secret, for these were halcyon days for anyone in the public eye. In 1987 there wasn't such a thing as an official 'celebrity' magazine, it would be another year before *Hello!* hit the stands in the UK, and, as it was, Melbourne was not exactly the obvious choice of hunting ground for the prowling paparazzi. If they wanted to get their big-money shot they were better off in LA, New York, London, the South of France, the Caribbean, Sydney even, for they weren't going to find what they wanted in the suburbs of Nunawading. Back in those days the concept of celebrity was completely different to what it is today: you actually had to *be* someone, you had to have earned your star status for the public to be interested in you. The Princess of Wales, Madonna, Tom Cruise, Michelle Pfeiffer, Cindy Crawford, Richard Gere – these were the faces that sold magazines back then; these were the people who held some kind of currency.

Kylie and I were well-known, there was no denying that, and we had our own little following in the television press in Australia, but we never for one moment thought of ourselves as celebrities, we were just two kids who acted for a living. We didn't really have to worry about being stalked by the press. Or so we thought.

A couple of months after we'd returned from Bali, a series of photographs of us on holiday together appeared in *The Truth*, an Australian tabloid. They were of us sitting on the beach in Kuta, and, much to Kylie's complete mortification, she had been photographed topless. 'ARE KYLIE AND JASON AN ITEM?' screamed the headline.

The story spread like wildfire, and, much to our distress, was followed up by everyone. As much as we wanted it to, it just wouldn't go away.

Unsure of how to handle the situation, I turned to Brian. 'Should we just come clean and admit to it?' I asked him. 'Maybe that way it will all just die down and they will leave us alone.'

'Errrrr, hello? Jason? *Are you there?* I sometimes wonder with you guys. Now listen to me. Say nothing, absolutely nothing. Direct all enquiries through me and I'll deal with it. Keep 'em guessing, keep 'em guessing. This is huge, Jason. Just huge. So roll with it, you hear me?'

Chapter Eight

Episode 523

I'M NOT SURE that any of us ever anticipated the phenomenon that *Neighbours* would become when we first started working on the show. Of course, we all knew that it had potential and hoped it would gain a solid fan-base over time, but none of us, not even the executives at the network, imagined for a moment that it would eventually rank as one of the most successful serials in the history of Australian television. However, that's exactly what happened. By the spring of 1987 *Neighbours* was riding high at the top of the television chart and, much to my surprise, it had gained a strong international following as well.

It was by no means unusual for television shows to be franchised abroad, for this is where the production companies make their real money after all, but what did amaze me was just how many countries wanted to sign up for their daily slice of Australian suburban life. In its twenty-year run *Neighbours* has been broadcast in over sixty countries, from Canada to Germany to Ireland to Japan, but the territory where it has always enjoyed its greatest success outside of Australia is the UK, and, although I didn't realise it at the time I played Scott, this would have a huge impact on the rest of my life.

I doubt the BBC realised just how popular the show would become when they bought the rights for it from Grundy's towards the end of 1986. I think they saw it as nothing more than a filler for their morning schedule, a show that might appeal to bored housewives or the elderly, and as such it was first broadcast just before the lunchtime news, and repeated the following day mid-morning. But, as time went on, *Neighbours* found a new, younger fan-base who caught the show when they were off from school or in between lectures at university. If television folklore is to be believed, Michael Grade, who was Director of Programmes at the time, was alerted to this fact by his daughter, and at her behest moved the morning repeat to the teatime slot of 5.35 p.m. so that children could come home and watch it after school. This new piece of scheduling was a master-stroke for Grade and the BBC, for within just a couple of months in its new timeslot *Neighbours* had gained a combined viewing rate of over fifteen million.

No one seemed to care that it was hardly the most sophis-ticated of dramas; that the acting could be a little rough around the edges, or the storylines were a tad farfetched, or that the sets wobbled. If anything that just added to the general appeal of the show. For some reason we appeared to be giving our audiences, at home and abroad, exactly what they wanted, and they couldn't seem to get enough of it.

'*Neighboursmania!*' is what Brian had dubbed it. 'It's huge!' he'd shout. 'Just huge!' And there was no denying the fact that he was right. You only had to go to your mailbox at the studio in the morning to realise the impact the show was having. Thousands of letters would arrive for us each week from our fans across the world. It got to the stage where our post no longer fitted into our pigeonholes and bags would have to be left for us in sacks in the hallway instead. The telephones at Channel Ten's press offices in Sydney and Melbourne would ring off the hook with requests for magazine and newspaper interviews, television appearances and so forth. We were constantly being bombarded with invitations to appear at parties, attend club evenings or film premieres. *Neighbours* fanzines started being published, souvenirs went into production; they even created a board game around the show. Not all of this was authorised by Channel Ten, who broadcast *Neighbours*, or Grundy's, who owned the show, either, but they certainly weren't getting hot under the collar about it. Imitation is always the highest form of flattery, and at the end of the day it all just promoted the show.

Such was the popularity of the soap that it became something of a showcase for people wanting to promote or advertise a product. In a scene you would only have to take a sip from a carton of brand-name orange juice and the following day cases of the stuff would be sent to the studios by its manufacturers in the hope that their juice would feature in the soap again. It took product placement to a whole new level and it became something of a joke within the cast. If you needed something for your home – an iron, a food processor, a power drill – then you only had to pick up the product for a couple of seconds when the camera was on you and it would be yours. I was once sent three Fender guitars as a present simply because Scott had mindlessly strummed away at one in a scene with Charlene.

But for all the perks that went hand in hand with starring in a successful television show, we soon discovered that there was a downside to it as well, something I first experienced when the photographs of Kylie and me holidaying together appeared in the press. And yet, as difficult as that had been for us, at the time we both realised we couldn't really complain. Although neither of us had got into the industry with the sole intention of becoming famous, the fact was that it went with the job description, and as long as we pursued our chosen career paths this would be something that we would have to learn to accept and deal with. But when it came to our families and friends it was another story. There were times when I felt quite awkward being out with my mates and knowing that people were looking at me, monitoring my every move, for all I wanted to be on those occasions was one of the boys, and yet it was almost impossible to fully relax and let my hair down. If we were out at a party in a club there was no way I could be seen to be misbehaving, even though I was just a teenage boy. So I wasn't a drinker, but I still enjoyed my pot, yet I knew that I couldn't be seen to be stoned because the public and press would have had a field day. I had to keep a lid on that part of my life.

Even going out for dinner with Dad and Marlene became something of an ordeal. It was always flattering to have people come up and say nice things about the show or my performance, but when I was out like this I never considered myself as anything but a part of my family. So when I was sitting in a restaurant and someone came up and said: 'Aren't you that kid from *Neighbours*? Scott Robinson?' I would find myself squirming in my seat. For at that precise moment in time I wasn't Scott from *Neighbours*, I was Jason Donovan, a nineteen-year-old boy trying to enjoy a quiet meal out with my stepmother and, in my opinion, my far more illustrious father. I knew that all this was hard on Dad. He had been in the business for nearly thirty years, he'd done his time, trodden the boards, earned his wings, received the prizes, the reviews and the accolades, and yet now I was the one getting all the attention and that made me feel very uncomfortable. When people came up to me when we were out I wanted to point to him and say, 'Don't you know who he is?' But I learned to hold my tongue. I'd give them a smile, thank them for their kind words and sign their piece of paper.

It was quite difficult for everyone, not least my younger brother Paul. His first days at school didn't go smoothly, which really upset me. From the moment he walked through the door and the older kids found out who he was related to, they pestered him throughout the day, asking questions about me. It took him a while to find his feet there and to discover who his real friends were, which must have been very frustrating for him.

As our public profiles grew, Kylie and I became more determined than ever to keep our relationship private. We both felt that it was important to hold something back for ourselves, and so on Brian's advice we carried on insisting in interviews that we were nothing more than friends. I can't pretend that it was easy for either of us, for when you are young and in love there is a natural desire to want to share that emotion with the rest of the world, to stand on rooftops and shout it out for everyone to hear. There were times when we both found it deeply frustrating, and we hated having to lie to people. I was proud that Kylie was my girlfriend, what man wouldn't be? She was young, talented, beautiful, artistic and funny. There was a part of me that wanted *everyone* to know I was with her, not least the thousands of male fans who wrote to her on a daily basis, but I felt that if I went on the record and told the truth, then I was opening a door that could never be closed.

I can't say whether it was the right decision to have made at the time. In hindsight I think that had we just come clean it might have made our lives a lot easier, but Kylie and I rather naively took the view that if we kept our silence then the public interest in our private lives would eventually die down. However, if anything it just added fuel to the fire. By refusing to be drawn on the state of play, we created an air of ambiguity over our relationship that just perpetuated the guessing game and caused further intrigue.

Kylie and I were always very conscious of the fact that we were part of an ensemble piece of drama and that the storyline we had together was just one part of a much bigger picture, but towards the middle of 1987 the romance between Scott and Charlene seemed to be taking on a life of its own. Fans couldn't get enough of the love story and the writers were taking this into account. Even though the two characters were still in their teens in the soap, it was decided that they should marry. The writers thought this was the only way forward for the couple, the perfect climax to their long-running courtship, and the producers knew that a big fairytale wedding between two of the show's most popular characters would be an absolute ratings winner.

It's quite strange really but I don't have many recollections about the 'big day' itself, other than I remember it being very long. Any scene that involved more than three characters was always difficult to shoot, so given the fact that the whole cast had to congregate at Holy Trinity Church, in Doncaster, to act as our wedding guests, it was quite complicated. It was a hot day and I felt pretty uncomfortable standing there in my tailcoat, for my collar was a bit tight, and Kylie spent most of the day trying to keep her dress clean. I have to say that she looked pretty damn good in it, but I am also willing to admit that it felt quite surreal seeing my girlfriend trussed up like that, and the two of us had to try to suppress our giggles as we stood at the altar and delivered our vows to one another.

The wedding of Scott and Charlene was to go down in television history. When the episode (episode 523) was aired in Australia on 1 July 1987, the ratings went through the roof, and when it was screened in the UK the following year, twenty million viewers sat down to watch it. It even made the cover of *Time* magazine back home in Australia. On the day it was first screened on Channel Ten, in a bid to drum up publicity, Brian decided to send Kylie and me to the Westfield Shopping Centre in Parramatta, Sydney. 'Big smiles!', 'Look loved-up!' were his tongue-in-cheek instructions – which would have been all well and good had we not had a lovers' tiff that morning – but we were both professional enough to leave our private dispute behind us as we got out of the car. Over four thousand fans had gathered there and it was complete madness. The producers had made a replica of Scott and Charlene's wedding cake, and when we leaned forward to cut it complete pandemonium broke out. A couple of fans fainted and several got hurt in the throng. I remember both of us trying to plead for calm, but it was no use because neither of us could be heard over their screams.

I had never seen anything like it. 'Scott! Charlene! We love you!' they kept calling out.

As we eventually made our way out of the shopping centre – and all the madness – a photographer took me to one side. 'So when are you going to do it?' he asked.

'When are we going to do what?'

'When are you and Kylie going to make it official?'

Chapter Nine

Sometimes You Kick, Sometimes You Get Kicked

WHEN YOU FALL in love for the first time you always believe that it is going to last forever. You cannot imagine for one moment ever being separated from the one you love, let alone countenance the day when they turn to you and say 'It's over'. You think, 'This is it, this is the real thing, they are the one', and as such you start planning your future together. Although I was a long way off from imagining Kylie and myself walking up the aisle to the sound of Angry Anderson's 'Suddenly', the rock anthem that had carried Scott and Charlene out of the Holy Trinity Church into a life of married bliss, I really did think at the time that we would be together for the rest of our lives.

There seemed to be such a connection between us, one that I believed could never be broken. We understood each other's work, and the pressures that it put us under; we had similar interests, shared the same sense of humour and adventure, and we liked each other's friends and families. Those first couple of years as a couple was like one long honeymoon. We took holidays together – as well as Bali, we went to Hawaii and Tahiti and took regular trips to Sydney. In Queensland we saw Whitney Houston play at the opening of Sanctuary Cove on the Gold Coast, and we spent time with Gran in the country or would go and visit Kylie's grandmother on regular occasions.

With Kylie's encouragement I even set about trying to form a closer relationship with my mother. Watching Kylie and Carol together I couldn't help but envy the bond they had between them, and although I was realistic enough to know that it was unlikely that Sue and I would ever have that, she was my mother and I wanted her to be part of my life. I wasn't a child any more and it felt slightly ridiculous for Gran to have to act as our go-between. If we were to form a proper relationship then I knew we would have to do it ourselves, so late one afternoon I summoned up the courage and called her. In a long and quite emotional conversation I told her how I felt and, much to my relief and, perhaps, surprise, she told me she felt the same way, and invited Kylie and me to come and see her the following week. I'm not going to pretend that this occasion was some grand reunion – mother and son running towards each other, arms outstretched Hollywood style – but on the subsequent afternoon we spent together we made a connection, and that meant a lot to me.

As strong as the bond between us was at that time, Kylie and I had our moments. I always like to think that I am pretty easygoing, but when something rattles me I can be fairly hot-headed, and she could be quite fiery when she wanted to be. So there were times when we really went for each other. None of our fights were ever very serious, but we were prone to the odd spat and would wind each other up; and while there were so many positives about working together, when we weren't getting on it could be difficult.

Of course, we were both professional enough never to let this interfere with our work, and when the cameras were rolling we gave it our all, and would act the loving couple if the script required it, but when the director called cut and we stepped out of character and off the set, we would give each other the cold shoulder. There are some people who relish confrontation and get off on verbal slanging matches, but I am not one of them. I'm the type of person who prefers to vent their anger by punching walls rather than sounding off, and I suffered from quite a few raw knuckles back then. I remember having such a row with Kylie in the car one day that I threatened to get out of it while it was still moving, but, as always, she managed to talk me round and within minutes we had made our peace. As heated as our fights could be, they never lasted very long. Sure, we would get irritated and annoyed with one another from time to time, but at the end of the day we loved each other very much, and neither of us was prepared to walk away from the relationship simply because we'd had a petty fight.

I used to think that had Kylie and I not worked in the profession that we did, had we been just a couple of kids from Melbourne with normal jobs and ordinary lives, then maybe things would have turned out differently for us, for there is no question that working in such close proximity to one another put an extraneous amount of pressure on the relationship. But with the benefit of hindsight I can see now that we were never really going to last the distance. The course of young love is never a smooth one as it is, and although I couldn't see it at the time, there was a world out there that we both needed to explore.

If I had to put my finger on what ultimately drove us apart then I would say it was music, which at the end of the day was quite ironic really, given that it had always been a mutual passion for us. We loved listening to all the bands, buying records together, going to gigs and concerts, dancing at the clubs in Sydney and Melbourne, and our karaoke sessions in my car. I always thought Kylie had a pretty good voice on her, and I wasn't the only one.

In 1986, a couple of months before we started seeing each other, Kylie had stunned the crowds at the Fitzroy Football Club when she performed a couple of numbers during their Giant Fightback Variety Night. With the help of some of the cast of *Neighbours*, who provided backing vocals, she sang a duet of 'I've Got You, Babe' with the actor John Waters and then finished with Little Eva's Sixties hit 'The Locomotion'. I'd seen Kylie perform before, for she had appeared in a couple of episodes of *Young Talent Time* alongside her sister Dannii, and she'd been good, but not as good as this. She was sensational and the crowd loved her.

'Fucking hell,' Alan said to me afterwards. 'That was amazing! Not only does she look like an angel but she sings like one as well.'

Alan was not alone in his admiration for Kylie that night. Greg Petherick, a producer at *Young Talent Time*, had been blown away by her. Though the performance had been less than polished, he recognised in an instant that she had star quality, and within just a couple of weeks he'd ushered her into Melbourne's Sing Sing Studios to record a demo of 'The Locomotion', which he forwarded on to his friend Amanda Pelman, a promotions manager at Mushroom Records.

As much as Kylie liked to sing and dance, I know that she never really thought for a moment that she could make it as a pop star back then. For her it was just about having a bit of fun, something she enjoyed. But that was the thing about Kylie – she never really had to try at anything, she was one of those people to whom things just come. The big cheeses at Mushroom weren't sure about Kylie at first. Because of *Neighbours* they knew who she was, but they didn't know she could sing, and I think that when Amanda initially suggested they sign her they had their reservations, unsure of whether she would be able to make the transition from soap star to pop star, but when they heard the tape for the first time they realised they'd struck gold. Within a week they had signed her and had her in the studios re-recording the song.

By the time 'The Locomotion' was released in Australia, in 1987, Kylie and I were already a couple and I had moved to my house in Burnley. Although I knew that Kylie would have some success with the song, I never expected it to be the hit it was, but within just two weeks of getting into the charts it went to number one and would stay in that position for nearly two months. I remember the day that Mushroom called to tell her the news. We were lying on my futon in Gibdon Street, which I would put down as one of my greatest furnishing fashion mistakes, for I never had a decent night's sleep on that bloody bed, when the phone rang. I passed the call on to Kylie and when she learned that she had got her first number one she was understandably excited.

'You are happy for me, aren't you?' she asked.

'Of course I am!' I replied, hugging her. And I was genuinely happy for her, but with that came a terrible sinking feeling, as if I knew that this was to be the beginning of the end for us.

Not long after the song went to the top of the charts, Kylie and I took a holiday to Tahiti. We had both been really looking forward to getting away from everything and spending some quality time together. Rather unimaginatively we had booked a holiday at the island's Club Med resort, and after we checked into our room, exhausted from the flight, we slumped onto the bed with the intention of getting a couple of hours' sleep. My head couldn't have been down for more than ten minutes when the music started. There was an exercise class going on right outside our balcony and the track they had decided to do their workout to, and to belt out at full volume, was none other than 'The Locomotion'.

As soon as I heard Kylie's voice instruct everyone to join her 'brand-new dance' and start swinging those hips, I groaned.

This is just marvellous, I thought to myself. Bloody marvellous! As into Kylie as I was, I didn't want to do the bloody locomotion! I wanted to sleep. I had come halfway across the world to get away from all that. All I wanted was to be with Kylie, my girlfriend – not Kylie the pop singer, or Kylie the actress. When I told her what had happened when she woke up she couldn't stop laughing. 'You have to admit it's pretty funny!' she said. I began to see the joke and get my sense of humour back, but the incident had made me see things for what they were. Whether I liked it or not, things were changing between us.

With her single doing so well in Australia, Mushroom knew that the next step for Kylie was to take her back into the studio and get her to record an album. They knew that it would fly off the shelves, the only problem was they didn't have any material for her. Kylie, unlike most acts in their catalogue, was not a singer-songwriter, she was a performer and they hadn't had time to work on anything for her. With its upbeat sound and catchy chorus, 'The Locomotion' had been the perfect song for Kylie, but who was to say that she would do so well with another cover. They knew they needed to find her material that had a similar vibe to 'The Locomotion', songs that would suit her vocal range yet were 'pop' enough to get the kids singing along on the dance floor, and they knew just the people for the job – Stock, Aitken and Waterman.

In the mid Eighties the music production team of Mike Stock, Matt Aitken and Pete Waterman were who you turned to when you wanted to get a top ten single. The trio were collectively known as the 'Hit Factory' thanks to their success and their brand of 'pop', the catchy music that dominated the British and European charts at the time. Rick Astley, Bananarama and Mel & Kim were just some of the acts to hail from their stable, and so Mushroom, who already had a licensing agreement with them, thought that they would work well with Kylie.

I guess it wasn't surprising that neither Matt, Mike nor Pete knew who Kylie was when she walked through the doors of their offices in London. Those guys were so prolific in those days that they rarely came up for air from the depths of their studios and when they did it was only ever to brainstorm over a game of table tennis. All Pete knew was that 'some little kid from *Neighbours*' needed some material for an album, but on the day itself it had completely slipped their minds.

'Kylie Minogue is here for you,' the assistant announced.

'Who?' Pete replied.

'Kylie Minogue – Mushroom Records – you were going to write some songs for her.'

'She should be so lucky!' he retorted.

'What did you say?' Mike said.

'She should be so lucky ...'

'That's brilliant!'

And so, as legend has it, Mike sat down and within just ten minutes had penned Kylie's first song.

'I Should Be So Lucky' was the first of a string of hits that would appear on Kylie's eponymous album, which was released in 1988. I have to confess, when she first played it back to me on her return from London and asked me my opinion, I ummed and ahhed, not really knowing what to say. It wasn't my kind of music – it was so obviously 'pop', annoyingly upbeat and unnervingly catchy, but for all my snobbery I could see that at the end of the day what Stock, Aitken and Waterman had produced was genius. Love it or hate it, 'I Should Be So Lucky' was a tune of its time. It was a song that suited her, and when we watched the first playback of her video I knew she was onto a winner.

And I wasn't wrong, for the moment it was released it not only soared to the top of the Australian chart but it matched itself in the British chart as well, and overnight, almost seamlessly, Kylie went from being a home-grown talent into an international star.

'You must be really proud of her,' Alan said to me on set one day. And, of course, I was. How couldn't I be? I loved her and wanted her to do well, and I knew how much this all meant to her, but at the same time her growing success was making me feel uncomfortable and, if I am going to be completely honest about it, I was jealous. I wanted to have what she had, I wanted the success and all that went with it. I wanted to be doing what she was doing. I wanted to have a music career of my own.

From a very young age I had always harboured a secret ambition to become a rock star – most boys do. When I was sitting at my drum kit at home in the living room in Union Street I fancied myself as something of a Ringo Starr; later, when I was going through my Kiss stage, I wanted to be Ace Frehley. At that time, more recently I'd looked towards the likes of Michael Hutchence – well, who wouldn't. It was the year of INXS's Kick Tour and he had to be, without a doubt, possibly the coolest man ever to come out of Australia. I'd been in bands, not that they'd ever come to much, and when I was alone at home I would often sit up late into the night penning music and lyrics as I strummed away at my guitar.

Dad always encouraged me to be musical, and now that I was acting he was keener than ever for me to keep up with it. He saw it as just another string to my bow. If you could hold a note then the world of musical theatre was open to you; if you could play an instrument all the better, for it might open other doors. 'Always try to be as versatile as possible,' he would tell me.

I knew that he was right, but I just didn't know how to go about it. Although I had appeared on *Young Talent Time* once, showcasing on that show wasn't really my style. I didn't have a manager and I didn't have a record company. I didn't even have a band, for there simply wasn't time to get one together outside of work. Some of the other cast members had formed one of their own – Guy Pearce was an extremely gifted saxophonist and Craig McLachlan was good on guitar – and for a time Kylie acted as their singer, but for some reason I never got involved. At that time my only real experience of singing live had been when I had taken part in a benefit concert for drugs awareness in the spring of 1987.

'You can't be serious!' James said to me when I'd told him I was in the line-up.

'Yes, why not?'

'Because it's called the "Say No to Drugs" Concert, and you just happen to be one of the biggest pot-heads I know,' he laughed. 'We don't call you Bongovan for nothing! It's hilarious.'

Uncertain of how I was ever going to make my big break into the world of music, I put my ambitions to the back of my mind and decided to concentrate on my acting instead. The Scott and Charlene wedding story had not only been a huge success with fans but it had caused something of a buzz within the industry as well. We were nominated for a series of television awards, and in 1988 we took home an armful of Logies – popular public-voted awards somewhat like the Australian equivalent of the BAFTAs. As well as winning a group trophy for Best Australian Drama, we were named Most Popular Actor and Actress, and Kylie, who had insisted on making her own dress for the occasion, took home the much-coveted Gold Logie. It had been quite a night for us, and when we got home we piled the statuettes high behind the bed.

'Don't you think we should go out and celebrate?' I asked her. I was on a natural high and I wanted to party.

'You know what, all I really want to do is go to bed! But you go if you want to go, I don't mind.'

I knew Kylie didn't like staying up late, but I'd thought she might make an exception on this occasion – she had just been crowned queen of Australian television after all. I tried to persuade her to change her mind but she was having none of it.

'Just go and have fun!' she told me. 'I'll see you later.'

With Kylie's star hurtling towards the stratosphere it was becoming increasingly difficult for her to juggle her dual careers. She was being pulled in so many different directions and there simply weren't enough hours in the day for her to do both music and television, and so that year she took the decision to leave the soap. Of course, I didn't want to see her go, but when we talked it through I knew that she was making the right decision. She had such a great opportunity on her hands and it was ridiculous to waste it. She no longer wanted to act, she wanted to be a pop star, and I supported her in that because I knew she could do it. And, as it was, I don't think the soap could really carry her any more. She had become such a star she was starting to become bigger than the show itself. When viewers watched her on screen they no longer saw Charlene Mitchell, the local mechanic, but Kylie Minogue, the pop star.

The producers were sad to see her go. She had been such a hugely popular character and they knew that they couldn't replace her. Ever hopeful that she might return to the show one day, rather than kill her character they sent her off to Brisbane where she was supposed to be setting up home for Scott, but when she walked off the set that day I think we all knew she wouldn't be coming back.

When Kylie told the producers she wanted to leave I think they were nervous that I might follow suit, but I had no intention of quitting just yet. 'Why bite the hand that feeds you?' was my attitude, but I did ask them whether I could have more free time to pursue other projects, and later that year I took a three-month sabbatical to work on a miniseries called *Heroes* in Queensland. It was a great role, and as much as I didn't want to be parted from Kylie for such a long period of time, I knew that I couldn't pass on this opportunity. I was happy on *Neighbours* but I also knew that I didn't want to play that role forever. I had to start thinking outside the box and consider my future. As it was, Kylie came to visit. She had been supposed to be shooting a new music video, 'It's No Secret', back in Sydney, but at the last moment she somehow managed to swing it so that it could be filmed in Queensland instead.

I was really pleased that she came, for it meant we could spend some time together at last. When she'd left *Neighbours* to concentrate on her music I'd rather assumed that she would have more free time, but if anything the reverse happened. If she wasn't in the recording studio or making her videos then she'd be having costume fittings or would be doing promotional work, interviews, photo shoots and television appearances. And if this wasn't enough, she had just won the lead role in an Australian feature film called *The Delinquents*. We still had our evenings together, but it wasn't quite the same, and I couldn't help but feel that her career was coming between us.

Our relationship had always been extremely equal, but I was beginning to feel that the dynamic was changing. It was no longer Jason and Kylie, Scott and Charlene, two people who worked as a team and as a couple. As her star grew, Kylie suddenly had this whole new identity, and that was quite hard to cope with. Kylie never brought her work home, instead it took her away, and I felt as though I was constantly having to compete for her attention with a team of virtual strangers, whether it was her manager Terry Blamey, the film production company, the executives at Mushroom, the guys at Stock, Aitken and Waterman, the press, or the millions of adoring fans she had gathered along the way. It felt more and more like something was going to have to give.

Chapter Ten

Idol Speculation

'IF YOU'RE GOING to get into the music business then you had better get yourself a manager, Jay,' Marlene said to me over coffee at Union Street. 'For if it's anything like the modelling world then you'll need someone good to represent you and look out for your interests. There are a hell of a lot of sharks out there, believe me.'

It was early 1988 and, try as I might, I'd been unable to let go of my dream of making it as a singer. If anything my ambition burned stronger than ever. 'If that's what you want to do then have a crack at it,' Dad had told me when I talked things through with him. He'd had a brief flirtation with the music industry himself when he'd released a single called 'Hickory Dickory Dock' in the Seventies, but I think the less said about that the better. 'All I'm saying to you is have a little faith in yourself. Okay, so you might not be ready for the Opera House, but you can hold a tune, play the guitar a bit, what are you worried about?'

I wasn't sure what was holding me back really. There was a small part of me that feared the knock-back but I'd worked long enough in the industry and learned enough lessons from Dad to know that I would just have to take that on the chin. If I got laughed out of the offices of a record company then hey, I still had the day job. I'd dust myself down and bounce back. 'If you don't try then you'll never know' was the motto in the Donovan house. Both Marlene and Dad had been supportive, although Dad wasn't convinced that I should turn my back on acting for good, for he thought that's where my strength lay.

Kylie had also been encouraging. It had taken me a while to broach the subject with her because I was worried that she might think I was treading on her toes, but she didn't see it that way at all. She of all people knew how into music I was back then, and she has always been a great believer in following one's instinct. 'Go for it,' she said.

And so, with my family's backing and Kylie's blessing, one balmy afternoon I found myself making my way to the offices of Richard East, one of Melbourne's finest music impresarios.

Now, Richard didn't handle solo music acts, and it had been quite a while since he'd managed a band either for that matter – and he'd spelt that out quite clearly during our first meeting. What Richard did for a living was to promote live shows for the likes of Jimmy Barnes and Dizzy Gillespie, and I have to admit that I did wonder why I had been sent to see him. In my pocket I had a long list of other people to see, who were not only just as reputable but were desperate to sign me up and cash in on my career, and yet here I was having an audience with a man who not only kept insisting that he didn't do management but who didn't have the faintest idea of who I was.

To be fair to Richard, while *Neighbours* was pretty huge back then I was under no illusions about my celebrity, and I did realise that not everyone had either the time or the inclination to sit down each evening and tune into the show. However, with all due respect it was on most people's radar. It was hard not to open a magazine or paper at the time, or tune into the radio or watch television, and not know who we were, but Richard didn't seem to have even heard of the show. It was as though it had completely bypassed him and he was living in some kind of parallel universe.

'*Neighbours* ...' his assistant Noleen tried to explain. 'It's a hit show, all the kids love it, and Jason is one of their most popular actors.'

Richard looked blankly at us both. 'I don't get it. I don't understand why you have come to see me. I don't want to be rude because you seem like a nice-enough guy, but I just don't see how I can help you.'

I was beginning to feel the same way myself, and had Marlene not passed his name on to me on the recommendation of her close friend Cathy, I would have been out that door there and then; but there was something about Richard that kept me in my chair, and after a couple of minutes in his company I knew I wanted to sign with him.

I have always been of the opinion that you can't buy style: you either have it or you don't, it's as simple as that, and Richard not only had it, he oozed it. Everything about him screamed 'cool', in a wonderfully understated way – from his sharply tailored suit, to his designer shoes, to his laundered, partly unbuttoned shirt. He wasn't flash, he wasn't loud, and there was nothing contrived about him; he was just very hip without even trying to be. Even his office was a work of art: with its gum-tree green wall and stylish furnishings it was the type of room that wouldn't have looked out of place within the pages of an interiors magazine. Being in his presence was like living and breathing the latest issue of *GQ*.

'What do you want me to do with you?' he asked.

'I'm looking for someone to manage my music career.'

'Have you got a music career to manage? Are you in a band? Where have you played? Do you write your own music? Do you have a demo tape? How would you describe your sound?'

Of course, I was unable to answer any of the above.

'But he's *Jason Donovan*,' Noleen volunteered.

Richard sat back in his Eames chair, put his hands behind his head and looked down at the papers on his glass desk.

'Let me think about it,' he said.

* * *

The longer Richard took to make up his mind to sign me, the more convinced I became that he was the right person for me. There were so many charlatans in that world, so many wide boys out there who were simply in for the kill. They didn't care about you as a person, they had no interest in what you wanted to do with your career, they just wanted to pimp you out, keep you working so that you could keep making them a buck or two. It wasn't about you as an artist, it was all about the colour of your money. I knew enough about Richard to know he wasn't like that. Sure, he was a businessman, and a good one at that, and at the end of the day he wanted to make money, but his past history also showed that he really loved the industry.

As well as his sense of style and his steely determination, I think what really swung it with me regarding Richard was the fact that, unlike so many people who were knocking at my door at the time, he didn't want to sign me just because I was a name – for if anything I knew that was probably stalling him in his decision. Sure, he realised that it had some kind of currency, but he wanted to be certain that there was something behind those two words, Jason Donovan – that I actually had something he could work with.

After a couple of weeks of sitting on the fence he eventually got in touch again, and to my great relief he told me that we had a deal. I'm not really sure why he decided to work with me, only he could answer that, but I know that Richard always thrived on a challenge and liked to keep on his toes.

'You're sure he's the right person for you?' Dad asked.

'One hundred per cent. I know he'll look after me and that I can trust him,' I answered. 'And you know the other thing I like about Richard? He looks like the type of guy I could catch a few waves with!' Dad laughed, but he also knew where I was coming from, for he always stressed the importance of being able to form a solid bond with those you worked with. That said, Dad maintained a healthy distrust for Richard, which was only natural. I think Dad always felt that he would like to handle my work and money, but I knew that wasn't a good idea.

When Richard called I was about to leave for Queensland to start filming *Heroes* so we didn't have any time to work on our strategy.

'What's the next step?' I asked.

'We'll talk that through when you get back,' he said. 'From now on just leave everything to me. I'll make some calls, put a few feelers out and see where that takes us.'

Richard was a man of his word, and when I got back to Melbourne he had already drummed up some interest from both EMI and Mushroom Records. My inclination was to go with EMI, purely on the grounds that Kylie was with Mushroom, but for that very same reason Richard favoured them and started to talk me round. He was also friends with Michael Gudinski, who was the MD of the company, and they had a good history of working together. As yet, nothing was concrete, but that suited Richard because he didn't want to rush into anything. His plan was to bide his time and generate some real interest in me as a music act before we signed on the bottom line. 'I'm thinking of taking you to the UK, to test out the market there,' he told me.

'But I haven't got any material yet!'

'That doesn't matter, you don't need any, it will be a PA tour. Let's get a bit of a buzz going, create a bit of a stir, that way we might get a better deal, create a bidding war.'

I could see where he was coming from, for it wasn't that dissimilar to what Brian had done with *Neighbours* in Australia, and Richard was astute enough to realise, having looked at Kylie's career, that we needed to capitalise on my popularity in the UK, for that was where the real money lay.

The plan was for me to appear at a selection of clubs and events up and down the UK. I'd arrive at the venue, get up on stage, say a few words to the crowd, throw in the odd joke about *Neighbours*, references to Kylie, Mrs Mangle and Bouncer and so on, and once I had got them going I would turn on my heel and be out of there. It was hardly very taxing work, and if it was going to help my career then I was up for it. In any case I was looking forward to the trip as I had never been to the UK, and I was especially keen to visit London. 'Don't forget to go to Kensington,' Dad boomed when I called him just before I left for the airport. 'You can check out where your cow-herding ancestors lived!'

Richard and I were both well aware that I had a following in the UK, but I think that we both underestimated quite how huge it was. I think Richard was especially taken aback. *Neighbours* had only been in his consciousness for a couple of months as it was, and until Noleen had given him the lowdown he had never even heard of Scott Robinson. So he was surprised to discover that each and every venue we visited was crammed to the rafters, and he was even more astonished when it became clear that most of the people who attended these events had come especially to see me.

'*Scott*,' they screamed hysterically. '*Scott! Jason! We love you!*'

'Bloody hell, Dono!' said Richard at our first gig. 'I had absolutely no idea ... This is going off.'

Our trip to the UK had been a fleeting one as I had to get back to *Neighbours*, but before we flew back to Melbourne Richard wanted to meet with the guys at Stock, Aitken and Waterman in London. He was now convinced that Mushroom was the right place for me to be, but he wanted me to meet with their writing team before I returned to Australia.

Despite all the success they had had with Kylie I know that Matt, Mike and Pete had some reservations about getting involved with me. It was nothing personal, they just thought twice about working with yet another *Neighbours* star, as they didn't want to get a reputation for that. However, they still gave me a chance, and when Pete heard the playback of a demo I'd finished recording with a producer at a studio off the Old Kent Road he was impressed. He'd only heard a couple of bars of the song when he shot his arm into the air, pulled it down as though he was working a slot machine, and in that great Warrington accent of his cried out: 'KER-CHING!'

'I tell you what, kid, I think we are about to make you very rich indeed.'

And with that the deal was done. Two days later I was in their studios in SE1 laying down my first single.

The track was called 'Nothing Can Divide Us', and it had originally been penned for Rick Astley, who, much to their obvious irritation, had just bolted from their stables. I didn't really like the song: it was a little high for me, I struggled with a couple of notes, and unlike the demo I hadn't been given much time to familiarise myself with the tune. To make matters worse, I knew that song had been meant for Rick, who, whether you liked his music or not, was a great singer. But somehow I got through it, and when I finished recording that day Pete patted me on the back. 'That's a hit!'

Of course, I was thrilled to have finally got my pop career off the ground, but there were moments when I wondered whether I had done the right thing. I liked the guys at SAW and Mushroom a lot, but there were times when I wasn't sure whether this was the best move for me. I'd always prided myself as something of a connoisseur when it came to music, and somehow I felt slightly uncomfortable about this whole process.

'Shouldn't I be writing my own songs?' I asked Richard one day.

He looked at me and smiled. 'That would be all well and good if you had spent the last ten years sitting in your bedroom developing a definitive sound of your own, playing at gigs and festivals, gaining a following, but you haven't. If you want to do that you need to have come up through the ranks, but if you want a pop career here and now you leave it to the experts. I know where you are coming from, Dono, but I am being realistic about this and trying to get you as much success as I can. Maybe you feel you are compromising your integrity, but in the end you will reap the rewards, you'll see.'

'Nothing Can Divide Us' entered the UK chart at number five in September 1988 and was number three in Australia. So it didn't go straight to poll position, but when you consider that I'd only been in the business for a blink of an eye it was a pretty respectable result, and I felt I could hold my head up high, even in my girlfriend's presence.

The following month Kylie and I took a trip to Sydney. It seemed an age since we had been together and we both felt like we could do with a couple of days off in Bondi. Richard didn't mind me taking a break. 'I'm heading there myself at the weekend for the INXS concert, why don't you two come along? It'll be a great night.'

I didn't doubt Richard for a moment. Since their incarnation INXS had always been one of my favourite bands. Us Aussies are a patriotic lot and we like to support our own, so it was only natural that I'd be a fan, but my admiration of them went far beyond a sense of national pride. In my mind these boys were *it*. They had this very innovative and distinctive sound to their music: it was rock, it was dance, it was raunchy, it was risqué, and it was raw. They were 'happening', as we used to say in the Eighties, but I think what really gave INXS that real '*it*' factor was their front man – Michael Hutchence.

Michael was the Mick Jagger of his generation: cool, hot, butch yet feminine, hard yet quite camp. He was a man of many contradictions and that gave him universal appeal: women wanted to bed him, men wanted to be him, and neither sex begrudged each other for how they felt. Everyone wanted to know him. When I told Kylie we had tickets for the concert at the Sydney Entertainment Centre she was delighted. Their 1987–88 worldwide Kick Tour had been met with critical acclaim and here we were about to share in that experience.

Ever resourceful, Richard had not only managed to get us the best seats in the house that evening, but he had arranged for us to have backstage passes as well, so when the show came to an end he asked whether we wanted to come and meet the band.

I'd expected it to be one of those meet-and-greet moments. There would be a quick introduction, we'd exchange a couple of pleasantries and then they'd be spirited away by their management, but Michael couldn't have been friendlier.

'Why don't you guys come and party with us back at the hotel?' he asked.

'Are you sure?'

'Yeah, why not? Unless you've got something better to do ...'

Something better to do? He had to be kidding.

And so Kylie and I accepted their invitation and agreed to meet Michael back at the Regent Hotel, where he and the band were staying. I remember there was quite a comic moment on the journey to the hotel. Kylie and I were sitting at the traffic lights in my Honda Civic hire car when the band pulled up alongside us in their massive limo. When they saw what car we were in they couldn't stop laughing.

I wasn't the only one to notice the buzz between Kylie and Michael that night. I'd noticed him staring at her when we met backstage, and when we got to his suite at the Regent he cornered her and they spent the rest of the evening locked in conversation with one another. He kept whispering in her ear and she was laughing. I didn't say anything at the time or try to intervene because I thought it was innocent enough, and in any case I realised that I would look pretty stupid telling Michael to back off as I dragged Kylie out of the party by her ear. When I mentioned it to Richard the following day he said that he'd picked up on it too. 'But I wouldn't give it a second thought,' he said. 'Michael is just an outrageous flirt who loves a pretty girl.'

Now I had proved that I could not only deliver a song but could sell a mountain of records in the process, I guess it seemed like a natural progression to have me team up with Kylie for a duet. There'd been a lot of talk about it at

Mushroom following the success of the single, and when they put the idea to Kylie and me neither of us was averse to it. We spent so much time singing to one another in private, we both rather liked the idea of having a go in public, and along with our management we knew that it would do well – as, thanks to the unerring popularity of Scott and Charlene, we had a guaranteed market for it. Once we had agreed to it, Mushroom didn't waste any time. They realised that any song by the two of us would be a strong contender for the Christmas market so they wanted to get it laid down as quickly as possible. With our schedules already bursting at the seams – I was filming *Neighbours* and Kylie was busy promoting her latest single – we didn't have time to fly to London to record the track with Stock, Aitken and Waterman. But no mountain was going to stand in their way, and so, armed with a love ballad Mike had written called 'Especially for You', Matt and Pete flew to Sydney instead.

Time was so tight we only had twenty-four hours to turn it around, and so we stayed up through the night until we finally had a product that they were happy with. Back in London the team set to work mixing the track, while we somehow managed to find a window in which to film a video for it. In its first week of release the song went straight to number two in Australia and number one in the UK, and would go down in music history as one of the biggest-selling singles of all time.

I remember feeling pretty damn good about life in general that Christmas. Even though Kylie and I had to suffer the indignity of having Cliff Richard knock us off the top of the UK chart – but hey, Christmas wouldn't be Christmas without his number ones – things were looking up. In terms of my career it had been a great year. I'd got a number one, and my solo single had done well. I'd enjoyed making *Heroes* and I'd won a Logie for *Neighbours*. Now that I was earning more money I had decided to move up the property ladder, so I had sold the house in Gibdon Street and made quite a tidy little profit from it.

I'd reinvested my capital in a property in Wellington Street, Richmond, and although it wasn't one of the best addresses in the neighbourhood it offered far more privacy than my last home. The house itself was a wreck, but that didn't matter to me as I planned to tear most of it down and start again. The reason I'd bought it was for the land, for it was set in the most wonderful garden with its own walnut tree, which the cockatoos would visit every morning. Gran had given me the name of her builder – John McCaffrey – while Marlene said she'd help with the interiors, and I had set about sketching designs for a conservatory, which I planned to build at the back of the house.

When I discussed my plans for the house with Kylie she looked excited and said she wanted to get involved, and that pleased me because I wasn't doing all this for myself. In my mind this was to be just as much her home as it was mine, because when the house was finished I wanted her to come and live with me.

Chapter Eleven

1989

FEW PEOPLE WERE surprised when I decided to quit *Neighbours* towards the end of 1988. As much as they hated losing central characters, the producers realised that after three years on the show I was ready to move on, and so they instructed the scriptwriters to start work on my final storyline.

I hadn't taken the decision to leave lightly. I had thought about it long and hard and had talked it through with Dad. I was aware that by walking away from the soap I was also walking away from a regular job and income, but I knew that was a risk I had to take and I wanted to leave on a high. To my surprise, Dad was fully behind my decision. He knew that if I stayed on the soap any longer I was in danger of getting typecast for the rest of my life, and he wanted me to make the most of the opportunities that lay ahead. Scripts were coming my way and there was talk of a film part, all of which he was eager for me to pursue, but I knew I wanted to concentrate on my music, and so, in January 1989, Scott Robinson bade his final farewells to his family and friends on Ramsay Street.

I felt quite sad walking off the set for the last time as we finished filming. *Neighbours* had been such a big part of my life and the cast and crew were a second family to me. Alan, Pearcy, Jonsie (Annie Jones), Brian, I was going to miss them all, but I knew I was doing the right thing. As fond as I was of my alter ego, I think I had taken Scott as far as he could go. I felt we were both in need of a fresh start, so it was time to consign his skateboard to the prop cupboard once and for all.

As much as I was going to miss him, I knew that Scott would be okay without me so I didn't feel that guilty. The scriptwriters were sending him to Brisbane to be with Charlene. After months of trying, the rookie journalist had finally managed to secure a transfer from the *Erinsborough News* to one of their local papers, and by all accounts I understand he is extremely happy there. I am not sure if he is an editor yet, but according to references made to him in the soap today all is well on the home front. His relationship with Charlene goes from strength to strength, and they are now the proud parents of two children, Daniel and Madison. And so I raise a glass to him, for there were moments when it was a bit touch and go for Scott, but at the end of the day that boy got his act together – far more quickly than I did, as it happened.

Richard was relieved that I was leaving the show – trying to juggle my music commitments round my filming schedule had proven to be a real headache, and he knew that if I was to enjoy success as a pop singer then I needed to focus on my game. I had an album coming out early in the year and there was a lot of work still to do on it. There were videos to be filmed, not to mention all the publicity that went hand in hand with the release of each single. This was by no means a part-time job, he kept telling me. To make it big we needed to launch a full-blown assault on the industry.

It was on Richard's instigation that I moved to London at the beginning of 1989. As the album was being recorded at Stock, Aitken and Waterman's studios, he thought it would be easier for everyone concerned if I was based there for the time being, as commuting from Melbourne to London at the drop of a hat was completely unviable.

A lot of my friends were taken aback when I told them the news.

'Moving to London? Are you crazy?'

'Sure it's fun for a holiday, but do you really want to *live* there full-time, when all your friends are here?'

'Do you actually know anyone in England, Dono?'

If truth be told, with the exception of Pete, Mike and Matt, and a few distant relatives in Ashford, I didn't really know anyone in England; but I wasn't too worried about that for I knew I would form some new relationships and pick up friends along the way. Having been raised as an only child I was independent by nature. I found that I could adapt to new situations quite easily and I liked meeting new people. I am the kind of person who always looks at the cup and sees it as half-full, not half-empty, and so I regarded the move not as hardship but as an adventure. This was a chance for me to broaden my horizons, and I was grateful that it had come my way. Of course I'd miss my friends back in Melbourne, and my family as well, but I wasn't going away for good and in time I would be back. My only consideration was Kylie, but due to work commitments she seemed to be spending far more time in Europe in those days than she did in Melbourne, so if I wanted to maximise my chances of seeing her it made sense to be in London. 'It's probably easier for both of us,' she said. 'We'll probably end up seeing more of one another.'

As it was, I wasn't going to be completely alone in London, for Richard was joining me for the ride, which I was grateful for. I knew it was a wrench for him because it meant leaving his wife and two young children back home in Melbourne, but we both realised I couldn't do this on my own. I needed his help and his guidance and – above all – his moral support.

And yet, as positive as I had been about the move, I couldn't help but feel a sense of apprehension as my car from Heathrow Airport drove into the centre of London. My last trip to the city had been so frenetic, so fleeting, that I hadn't really had a chance to take in my surroundings, but as the Daimler that had been booked to collect me slowly

Above Jason Mania hits the UK! Fans were screaming and fainting every 20 seconds – it was crazy!

Above A PWL roadshow. Pete didn't think touring was good for artists in terms of time and energy. He felt that was better spent on publicity and recording. Touring was too taxing. But I got a real buzz out of it.

Right Nice matching cycle shorts! This was at the sunset of my relationship with Kylie, around the time of her second album. I think I'd just had a go at the pap who took this photo as my tolerance levels of privacy invasion were at boiling point.

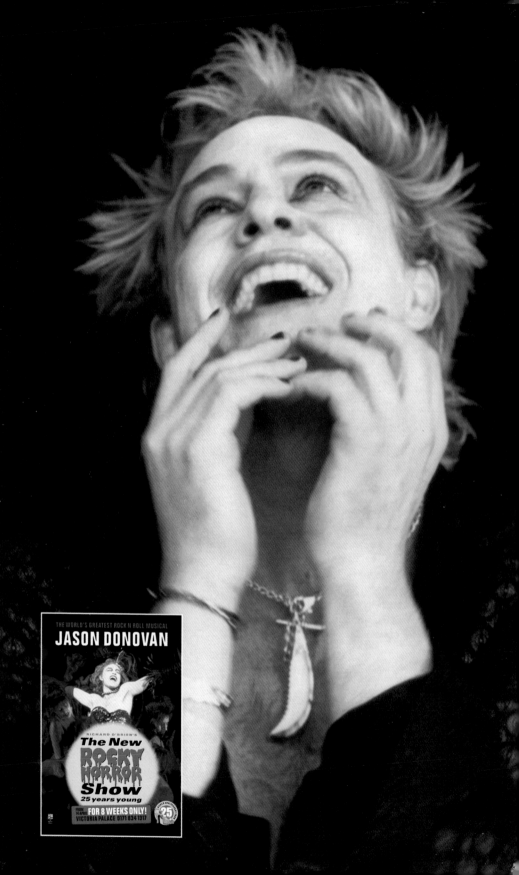

Left Ben Mendhelson and me in Bondi in the mid Nineties.

Below Avignon, France. Erica and I took a very long journey with Johnno and Claire to the Cannes Film Festival. I needed those dark glasses as I was pretty out of it.

Opposite Rocky Horror Show, 1999. I love to be dangerous on stage and the character of Frank gave me that opportunity. I also believed I looked fantastic in suspenders and was born to play this role! What a wonderful opportunity to cross-dress and be paid. I tended to play characters close to my own personality at the time. This was no exception.

DON'T TELL ANYONE, STAR BEGS HOST

Jason's legs turn to jelly in the deli

JASON DONOVAN'S partying caught up with him again yesterday when he collapsed in public for a fourth time.

The singer and actor — who has admitted taking cocaine in the past — was semi-conscious and trembling as he arrived at a Sydney hospital.

He recovered within 30 minutes and insisted on checking himself out, ordering: 'Don't tell anybody.'.

Donovan, 27, had been in a delicatessen near his Bondi Beach apartment. As he waited for his take-away pasta lunch, he slumped to the floor, banging his head on a fridge. Shop assistant Vicky Marks said: 'He was shaking like a leaf.'

A friend later insisted: 'Jason's fine — he's just been having too many late nights.'

Life in the fast lane: Donovan with his girlfriend Erica Baxter, 18.

Do

Left Me with a cocaine smile. I am not proud of these times but it's a lesson to all. Cocaine is for losers.

Right Chords of truth. This was a great holiday in Bali with Paul. I rented a villa, bought a motorbike, gave myself a Mohican, got a suntan and ate plenty of Nasi Goreng.

Below Jonathan, Mark Gerber and Kylie on Johnno's bike at the back of my Bondi apartment.

Above I'm lucky to be alive. This particular seizure was witnessed by Jonathan and another close friend of mine from Melbourne, Brett Goldsmith. The expression on their faces was, 'Mate, we are really worried about you' and became synonymous with my drugs period.

Left Smoking a doobie on the bed at Bondi.

EX-NEIGHBOURS STAR HOSTS GAY SHOW

How Jason swopped the Technicolor dream for a bin liner

By STEVE BUSFIELD
Showbusiness Reporter

HIS clean-cut looks and boyish charm made him a teenage girl's dream.

They rushed home from school to watch him on Neighbours, fell in love with his records and then queued up to see him in the spectacularly successful musical Joseph and his Amazing Technicolor Dreamcoat.

On Sunday night, Jason Donovan had a different audience.

The 27-year-old Australian was at the Astoria club in London, hosting his Gay UK, a benefit concert for Aids.

The technicolour dream seemed only a faint memory as Donovan, wearing an old T-shirt and wandered the 30 continents.

Later, he returned to the stage clad in a black bin liner and Dr Marten boots. He is said to have told the audience that he 'fancied a change'.

The singer agreed to host the concert after Robbie Williams, the former Take That star, dropped out.

Organisers of the event, which attracted an audience of 2,500 – are threatening to sue Williams.

There was none of the swooning that used to accompany Donovan's appearances. At the height of his fame he took the starring role in the musical that ran for two-and-a-half years at the London Palladium, pulling in £46.3million in ticket sales.

Indeed, there was some backbiting from the audience about his victory over The Face magazine, which he sued in 1992 for suggesting that he was a homosexual.

And when two of the contestants were asked to sing, they chose songs from Joseph, the show which gave Donovan his 1991 Top Ten hit, Any Dream Will Do.

'Jason did a lovely job as host,' said a spokesman for the event.

Donovan first tasted fame at 17, when he joined Neighbours, the Australian soap opera which also launched Kylie Minogue's career. In 1988, their duet, Especially for You, reached No 1 in the charts and cemented his place as a teenage pin-up idol.

But he has become just as well known for his health problems as he raced over the past two years. He has collapsed publicly four times — usually in clubs.

Last year he was due to star in a musical version of Billy Liar but the show was postponed. He recently returned to the stage in a revival of Camelot and is said to be rehearsing for a Rocky Horror Show tour.

Clean-cut hero: As Joseph in the musical

Friendly Neighbour: With Kylie Minogue   Stamping out a new image: Jason on Sunday   Picture: EDWA

Left After a two-day binge, I did a gig at the club night G.A.Y. For some reason I decided to put a bin liner on as an encore costume. I remember I hadn't slept for two days prior to doing this gig, which wasn't that uncommon. I had little care for what the press wrote about me in those days.

Right Erica and me. I always love a good wig. Was it fancy-dress or just a normal night out...?!

Above One of my many escapes from the London Palladium in 1991. This was a time when even getting out the stage door involved police protection.

Above Just after I had won the libel suit against *The Face*. I was ambushed by militant gay protesters who thought my actions were that of a homophobe. Not a particularly nice experience.

Above Singing 'Close every door to me' complete with loin cloth, heavy eyeliner and the classic drama school hand gesture. I can almost smell the glue the wigmaster applied to that biblical mullet each night.

Above One of my own. I love the simplicity of this and the smudging effect of the water that was accidentally dropped on the sheet and enhances the composition.

This is me in cocaine, cannabis, lipstick, smudging reds, eyeliner, snot, words. I'd use anything to try and express myself at this point. I'm not sure what I am trying to express, though – don't try to analyse it!

Peter Mac's photo of me in a Morrissey Edminston t-shirt, taken in Melbourne in the early Nineties. Mac captured me like no one else could. This photo became the image of me post *The Face* case.

made its way through Shepherd's Bush towards the West End, I realised just how alien this town was to me. One of the first things that struck me was just how low the buildings were. It didn't have the high-rise landscape of either Sydney or New York, where I had recently been. The second thing that got to me was just how bloody cold it was. The last time I had been in the UK it had been early autumn, and it had been relatively warm, but it was January now, and although we had seasons back in Melbourne I'd never experienced a full-on English bleak mid-winter. There was an icy chill to the air and the wind bellowed around me as I unloaded my cases from the car. It was summer back in Australia. All my friends would be heading down to the beach, they would be swimming in the surf, catching the waves, feeling the sun on their backs, smoking spliffs, and planning the barbeques they would have that night. For a brief moment I felt quite homesick and wondered whether I had made the right move, but I quickly came back to my senses.

However, I couldn't deny that it all felt quite unreal. I'd flown to London first class and had sat next to one of the most important men in Australia, the Foreign Secretary Gareth Evans. And as the stewardess had leaned over to ask me whether I would like a glass of champagne with my caviar, I'd realised just how crazy my life had become. In other people's eyes I might have been famous, this star in the making, but as far as I was concerned I was still a kid from the suburbs.

I knew that if you wanted to achieve things in life then sacrifices had to be made. There would be other summers in Australia to enjoy, a lifetime of beach parties and barbeques ahead of me, but I only had one crack at making it in the music industry. As Richard kept telling me, if that's what I wanted from life, I had to strike now. And, in any case, it wasn't such an ordeal. Through some pretty hardcore negotiating Richard had insisted to both Mushroom and Stock, Aitken and Waterman that if I came to London he wouldn't have me staying in some starless motel. If I made the move then they would not only have to rent me an apartment for the duration of my stay, but it had to be in one of the best areas in the city. Not for one moment had I ever questioned Richard's skills as a negotiator, but when I opened the door to the flat in Wilton Crescent, in the heart of London's Belgravia, my jaw dropped as I realised just how good he was. It was extremely elegant and quintessentially English – I had never seen anything like it.

Within days of arriving in London I was holed up in Stock, Aitken and Waterman's studios in SE1 adding the finishing touches to my first album, *Ten Good Reasons*. The hours were long and the team worked me hard, but I knew that it was going to be worth it in the end. They had written some really great material for me, including a track called 'Too Many Broken Hearts'. Unlike 'Nothing Can Divide Us', this song had been written especially with me in mind, and it suited my vocal range so I started to feel slightly more confident about my abilities.

The next step was to get to work on the cover, and so I was sent to the studios of Lawrence Lawry, a well-known photographer, famous for his portraits. I'm not sure why, but for some reason the shoot didn't go well that day. It was strange really, for I'd grown so used to having my photograph taken that I was normally quite comfortable and relaxed sitting in front of the camera, but that afternoon I felt terribly self-conscious and just couldn't get into it. When it became apparent to everyone on the shoot that it just wasn't working, Lawrence decided to call it a day.

'Let's wrap it up here,' he said. 'There's no point in carrying on, we'll try again tomorrow.'

I felt guilty that I had let everyone down and wasted his time.

'Don't worry about it. Believe me, it happens to everyone from time to time. Do you enjoy the odd, you know … smoke, to unwind? I'm going to have one. Jason, I think we could both do with one, don't you?'

'A smoke?'

'Yeah. Got some nice Cornish homegrown … what do you think?'

'Yeah … sounds perfect!'

That afternoon I made my first proper friend in London. In the months I had been in town I'd met countless people but I hadn't really bonded with any of them (there hadn't been time), and as much as I enjoyed and was grateful for Richard's company I was starting to feel quite alone. I'd always been quite a social person and I realised I wanted and needed some proper mates – people I could have a laugh with or turn to when I was feeling low, friends I could relax around. I felt I could be myself when I was with Lawrence, he was a similar soul. He spent time with Richard and me in Wilton Crescent, we hung out in his flat at weekends, getting stoned, and he introduced me to London. He took me to bars and restaurants and we spent evenings at the Chelsea Arts Club with his friend the photographer Charlie Roth. Thanks to him I was finally beginning to find my feet and feel at home in London.

With the album put to bed and nearing its release date, it was decided that I should go out on the road and join Stock, Aitken and Waterman's other acts on a tour of the UK. Like Brian and Richard, Pete Waterman understood how to play the game. If you wanted to get the kids on side, and get them to buy into the brand, then you had to give them something back in return – and he knew that there was nothing they liked more than an audience with one of their idols, so he devised a roadshow based on the old Motown Revue. The idea was to take us round the country and have us perform in front of a crowd of our adoring fans. The venues were never very big, but that was part of the plan. Pete didn't want us performing in half-empty stadiums, he wanted the clubs and venues he booked for us to be crammed to their full capacity. He wanted to create an electric atmosphere, get everyone into a real frenzy. Only too aware of how young his market was, these shows were staged for late afternoons so that the kids could be at home in bed on time, and he persuaded them to turn up with the promise of free soft drinks and burgers.

Big Fun, London Boys and Sonia were just some of the performers on the billing, and with Kylie out of the country it was decided that I was going to be the headline act.

Having done so many personal appearances during my time on *Neighbours* I was only too aware of how popular these events could be, but despite this I simply wasn't prepared for the reaction I got on this tour: it was complete and utter madness. Already pent-up from watching the other acts perform before me, when I walked out onto the stage the crowd broke into a frenzy. Girls screamed, cried and fainted. It got to the point where we had to make sure that there was an ambulance on standby outside each venue. 'Jasonmania' the tabloids called it, and Pete was delighted for it was exactly the reaction he was trying to get. 'Tell you what, kid,' he said to me with a broad grin after one of the shows. 'This is going to do absolute wonders for your career!' And he was right, for when my album and single were released in May they both went straight to the top of the charts, and would result in me becoming the highest-selling recording artist in the UK that year.

Kylie came to London that summer and we had a good couple of weeks together but it was over all too soon. I wished that we had more time together, but our work commitments had to come first. I was busy promoting the album, which was taking me all over the UK and Europe, and she was in the middle of her promo tour. Rarely were we ever in the same place at the same time – even in the same continent for that matter. At the end of the summer Richard had arranged for me to travel to America, and so I took the opportunity to meet up with Kylie in LA, where she was working, and we planned a short break together.

From the moment I met up with her at the Mondrian Hotel in LA I knew that something was up. She was normally so bubbly, so energetic, so pleased to see me, but she seemed quite subdued that day, like she was out of sorts. At first I put it down to the fact that she was tired. Kylie always loved her sleep and I knew that all this travelling was taking its toll on her. But as the days went on I realised that it was something far deeper than that. She was distant and removed. We were always so affectionate with one another but she didn't seem to want me to come near her. When I asked whether she was all right she would tell me that she was fine, but I knew she wasn't. When I tried to find out whether it had something to do with me, if I had said or done something that had upset her, she said no. But as much as I wanted to believe her, I couldn't. There was no denying that there was an atmosphere between us, a cold-ness, a stiltedness to our conversations, and as much as I tried to compensate for all of that, to try to make things better, I just couldn't. No matter what I did, or what I said, she didn't really want to know. It was as though she had drawn down the blinds and didn't want me in.

After four days together we said our goodbyes. She was flying west to start on the Asian leg of her promo tour, while

I was going north to join Richard in New York. We were going in different directions, both physically and mentally it seemed. As we got ready to leave the hotel my instinct was to call Richard and cancel the trip. I'd follow Kylie to the Far East and try to get our relationship back on course. But I knew I couldn't do that. For months Richard had been trying to find an inroad into the American market, and at last he'd made some headway. There had been a favourable response to 'Too Many Broken Hearts' and some talk of a record deal, and Richard knew that if he could get me air-time on the radio networks the battle was half-won. I realised that he couldn't do this on his own, for if we were to drum up any kind of interest he needed me there by his side. So, with a somewhat heavy heart, I boarded my plane to JFK.

I'd been in New York for a day when Kylie called me from Japan. There is little point in trying to recount the whole conversation, for all I can remember and could hear at the time were the words 'It's over'. It was like a blow to the stomach. I know that I tried to reason with her, tried to get her to change her mind, but she wasn't having any of it, she had made her mind up and it was final. I know I became quite emotional, that I veered from distress to anger, but it was to no avail. She would and could not be moved.

I'm not sure how the conversation ended. I remember trying to call her back, and Carol answering the phone and that our exchange was quite awkward. Kylie wouldn't come to the telephone, she said, for she felt there was nothing more to say.

I hung up and called Richard. He came straight to my room with Gary Ashley, the MD of Mushroom Records, who was out in New York on business. They both tried to calm me down but it was no use, I was distraught and inconsolable. I felt like my life had ended there and then, and I didn't know how I was ever going to recover. How could she do this to me? I kept asking. Why was she ending it? We'd been so happy together, so right for one another. Why was she throwing it all away?

I looked to Richard and Gary for answers but they said nothing. What could they say? I got on the phone to Australia, rang Gran and talked it through with her. She listened patiently to me and tried her best to comfort me. As much as I loved him I knew Dad would be pretty useless at a time like this, so I called Marlene, who was deeply sympathetic.

'It's only natural to feel hurt, Jay. Breaking up with some-one is always painful, and the fact that she was your first real love makes it all the more so, but you will get over it eventually. Time is a greater healer and you will come out of this a much stronger person. Trust me.'

If it hadn't been for the support I got from Richard, Gary, Gran and Marlene during that period I am not sure how I would have coped, for I felt completely destroyed and I couldn't imagine ever being happy again. Richard and Gary tried to keep my mind off things – and I remember blowing a serious amount of money in a clothes shop one afternoon – while Gran and Marlene kept in regular telephone contact. I tried to get Marlene to fly out to New York to be with me, but she couldn't because she had to look after Paul. Instead she'd sit on the telephone with me for hours at a time, telling me it would be okay, feeding me snippets of her life philosophies and trying to bolster my shattered ego. 'When all hope has gone, and you are at your lowest, what a wonderful opportunity to start over again,' she told me.

Kylie never did give me a reason for our break-up when she told me it was over. I'm not sure whether I asked her if there was someone else – if I did she didn't tell me, for I remember it was Richard who broke the news. Whether she had started seeing Michael Hutchence while we were still together is something I can't say, but she was very much with him now, and when I learned that, I understood that it was well and truly over between us and I would never get her back. How could I possibly compete with Michael? It was a battle I could never win.

Marlene was right, time is a great healer, and in the months that followed I gradually began to piece my life back together. I am not going to pretend for an instant that it was an easy time for me, because it wasn't. I still missed Kylie and there were moments, particularly when I was holed up on my own in some anonymous hotel room in a strange country, when I longed to hear her voice at the other end of the telephone, telling me she had made a terrible mistake. But, deep down, I knew that was never going to happen, and I just had to accept the situation for what it was: it was over and she wasn't coming back. She was with someone else now and, try as I might, there was no escaping that fact, for every time I seemed to open a newspaper or magazine during that period there they were together, laughing, smiling, holding hands, lovingly gazing into each other's eyes, being feted as Australia's new golden couple. Every image I saw of them together was like salt rubbed into my still-open wound, and yet I knew I couldn't hold her to blame, for as hurt as I was by the way our relationship had ended, I was coming to see that things hadn't been right between us for some time. Whether I liked it or not, our love had run its course.

It was a tough time emotionally for me – worse still having to see pictures of Kylie and Michael splashed across the press – but I could hardly take that out on her either. From the moment the media got wind of the fact that Kylie was now seeing Michael they hounded her. One British tabloid was even rumoured to have put out a £50,000 reward for the first picture of them together, and I knew from past experience that Kylie would have been feeling uneasy about the interest in her private life. She may have spent most of her life in the spotlight but she was always almost blissfully confounded by her own celebrity. As she saw it, she was just a girl from Melbourne who happened to act and sing and dance. Even when we were together she'd laugh when people tried to take photographs of us or when they would stop and stare at us as we went about our daily lives. Kylie and I had been lucky. We had successfully managed to keep our relationship private, but this time it was different – for everyone knew that Australia's favourite sweetheart had fallen in love with its most famous rock star. It was big news. Everyone wanted a piece of their love story. Everyone, that is, except me.

Chapter Twelve

Hard Yakka

KYLIE AND I kept our distance for a time. Other than a brief and slightly awkward moment when we met up at a studio to record our vocals for Band Aid II's 'Do They Know it's Christmas' we managed to avoid one another. I think we both realised we needed our breathing space, but in the December of 1989 I was touched when she invited me to the London premiere of *The Delinquents*. I momentarily thought twice as to whether I should go, but soon realised I had to be bigger than that. Whatever had happened between us at the end of our relationship was now water under the bridge; I was not going to throw away three years of friendship with Kylie over it. She might not have been my girlfriend any more, but that didn't stop me from feeling great affection or admiration for her, and I knew how hard she had worked on that movie and what it meant to her, so I accepted the invitation. However, as magnanimous as this gesture was, I still had my pride. There was no way I was going to cut a forlorn figure on the red carpet that night. Oh no. I was coming armed for the occasion.

Denise Lewis was the absolute antithesis of Kylie in every way. She was tall, buxom and, being that much older than me, she appeared quite worldly wise. She had been born and bred in Texas and had held on to her seductive Southern drawl; and when we first met she was at the top of her profession as one of the world's leading models. I may have still been nursing a broken heart, but I couldn't help but feel an attraction to Denise.

We had been introduced to each other by Lawrence at the Royal Albert Hall, when we had gone to watch a star-studded performance of The Who's rock musical *Tommy*. Elton John and Phil Collins were performing alongside Roger Daltrey that night, but I found it hard to focus on the show, mesmerised instead by the vision who'd been strategically seated beside me. At the end of the evening I asked Denise whether I could see her again, and to my amazement she agreed. We had dated on a couple of occasions and so it felt natural to ask her to the premiere. Denise knew what had happened between Kylie and myself, and had been a great support to me during that time, helping restore my confidence and sense of self-worth – and on the night of the screening she didn't let me down either. When we stepped out of the car at Leicester Square she took my arm and strode down that red carpet like it was her very own catwalk. As petty as it sounds now, I felt as though I had not only saved face but had scored a point.

Without wanting to be ungallant, for I liked Denise very much and had a wonderful time with her, I think I knew from the start that our relationship was never going to become serious, for I simply wasn't ready to fall in love again. Richard was well aware of my state of mind and encouraged me to throw myself into work instead.

If 1988 had been Kylie's year then 1989 was mine. So I may not have been the credible musician I wanted to be, but heck, at the end of the day I was the top-selling recording artist in the UK. My album had gone platinum within its first week and I had not only conquered the European markets but I was making serious waves in Asia too.

Only too aware of how fickle the industry was, and that I was in danger of having a very short shelf-life, Richard wanted me to capitalise on my success. I had to strike while the iron was still hot, he kept telling me. I couldn't afford to take a break, for if I took time out now, then when I came back who was to say that my fans wouldn't have moved on, or – as Richard liked to joke – grown up.

I was fully aware of my limitations as a pop singer. I may have been one of the biggest-selling artists of the time, but that had very little to do with either my voice or my music. Put it like this: you don't sit down in the evening and think 'I must listen to Jason Donovan's *Ten Good Reasons* again', in the way you might revisit George Michael's *Faith*, Madonna's *Like a Prayer* or one of Prince's early albums.

The chances are that if you ever did own one of my records you donated it to the charity shop at around the time your braces were removed and you landed your first proper boyfriend. My success was due to a combination of factors – the popularity of *Neighbours*, the fact that I was accessibly but not threateningly good-looking, and a team of highly skilled producers. That's what gave me currency.

Having spent much of his career producing live music shows, Richard was keen for me to go on tour. He knew from my record sales alone that it had the potential to be a sell-out and that together we could build foundations for the future and, at the same time, make a serious amount of money. At first I was unsure. For starters, despite my broken heart, I was beginning to enjoy life again. For tax reasons I had to prove residency in the UK and so I had just bought my first property in London – a penthouse flat in Chepstow Villas. Although I hadn't exactly been slumming it, after years of living in rented accommodation I finally felt at home, and I loved that apartment from the moment I walked through the door with the estate agent. It was light, airy and spacious; it had its own private lift that took you right up into the core of the apartment, and it was in my favourite neighbourhood, Notting Hill. At weekends, if I wasn't booked to appear on some Saturday-morning kids' show, I'd wake early, smoke a little joint and then take a stroll down the Portobello Road, where I'd buy my fruit and veg from the market stalls, meet with friends and stop for coffee. It was like being back on Bondi – all that was missing was the sea, to echo a George Michael 'Club Tropicana' lyric. I was proud of my new home and took great pleasure in getting it together, just as I had done with my first property in Richmond. I'd throw impromptu parties, and if friends came over from Australia I would have them to stay, which I have to admit became something of a nightmare for me after a while, as I felt like I was running a hostel.

But it wasn't just my life in London that was holding me back from the idea of touring. If I'm honest I was worried about whether I was up to it, for I didn't have that much experience of singing live. Back in those days we did a hell of a lot of miming. Whether you were appearing on television or doing personal appearances, you'd get up on stage, someone would flick on the track and you'd stand there and mouth all the words. So long as you didn't forget the lyrics, and there were those who did, then you couldn't go wrong. It was pop-singing by numbers. I remember saying to Richard on the day when *Top of the Pops* announced they were going live, 'Fuck, that's it, I'm done for, career over.' I was joking, of course, but not entirely. A year earlier, when I had been promoting *Ten Good Reasons*, I had been invited onto a major prime-time TV show in France. In rehearsals the producer, who I remember had one of those tiny fluffy dogs that only the French seemed to have, told me that once I completed the interview I would then move to the centre of the studio and sing.

'It'll be live, of course,' he told me.

'Live?'

'But of course!' he said, with a certain amount of Gallic indignation, his baguette well and truly up his arse.

I flashed Sally Atkins, the PR representative with me, a sideways glance. 'I guess I can do the verses but I'm not sure about the chorus. It's a little high for me,' I whispered. Sally was only too aware of the fact that this was a real issue for me, and so she talked the producers round and, to my shame, convinced them to let me mime.

It wasn't that I couldn't sing – I could – it was just that sometimes I couldn't cope with the musical range in the songs that Stock, Aitken and Waterman were giving me. I think it would be fair to say that Mike and Matt weren't writing the music with the intention of it being sung live, they were writing to sell singles. If a song was either too low or too high for an artist it would be ironed out in the studio. Once you had finished laying down a track the boys would spend hours working their magic with it until they finally had a product they were happy with. It was a long process, as they didn't have the computer technology there is today, and they would work reel-to-reel tape, in analogue, until they got it right.

I was by no means the only artist within that stable whose music had to be reworked. The fact was that Stock, Aitken and Waterman really *was* a hit factory. They were churning out hit after hit, day after day, and they simply didn't have the time to sit down and work with the artists, which it might be argued was to be their great undoing in the years to come. Had they spent more time developing their acts, I believe that the currency of their catalogue would be far greater today, for by spreading themselves so wide they ended up with a lot of one-hit wonders.

When I voiced my concerns about live shows to Richard he told me not to worry. 'The people coming to see these shows are there because of you,' he said. 'It doesn't matter if you are slightly off-key here and there, your fans aren't going to worry about that, all they want is to see you live. I think you should do it, because if it doesn't happen this year who's to say that you'll get another chance. If you are going to move forward you have to make this leap, no matter how terrifying it seems.'

And so, in the spring of 1990 I went on the road. Richard had teamed up with the legendary rock impresario Harvey Goldsmith, and together with my agent, Dave Chumbley, they planned a tour, which would kick off in London, take me to Europe and Asia, and would end with an arena tour of the UK. Within weeks of announcing the tour, tickets had sold out and more dates had to be added to the itinerary.

I knew from my record sales that I had a strong fan base, but even I was surprised by just how far and wide my net had been cast. I had dates in Budapest, Austria, France, Germany, Finland, Denmark and Switzerland, to name but a few. In the summer I would be travelling to the Far East to play in Thailand, China, the Philippines and Indonesia. The only place I wouldn't be playing was Australia. Although I'd had some chart success back home – I had number one singles there, after all, and a successful album – the public perception of me was that I was an actor first and foremost, and they hadn't exactly warmed to my new incarnation as a pop star. They liked their music acts to come up through the ranks. Michael Hutchence of INXS, John Farnham, Jimmy Barnes of Cold Chisel, Midnight Oil, The Divinyls, Hoodoo Gurus – I wasn't any of them, but that didn't bother me and I was the first to admit it.

Having got over my initial reservations about touring, I became excited about the prospect of going on the road. My personal life might not have been in great shape, but things couldn't have been going better as far as my career was concerned. In March we celebrated the launch of my second album, *Between the Lines*, a title that I can't help but find faintly comic now, given what was to become of me later on. And there would be a succession of hit singles to follow that year – 'Hang On to Your Love', 'Rhythm of the Rain', 'Another Night', culminating with a guest vocal on the Band Aid song 'Do They Know it's Christmas' and the hit 'When You Come Back to Me' in December 1989.

Richard had convinced me that going on tour would help take my mind off things, and to an extent he was right. Keeping busy was key to my recovery, but there were times when I felt quite alone. Long hours spent on tour buses, at airport terminals, in hotel suites and dressing rooms gave me time to reflect on my situation. Kylie was becoming a distant memory to me and I was moving on, but I still felt a void in my life. I wasn't missing her so much any more as much as the relationship itself. For over two years Kylie and

I had been joined at the hip. We worked together, we went out together, we seemed to spend every waking hour with each other. We understood each other like no one else could, and I sometimes wondered whether I would ever be able to find that again.

I longed to have that sense of security and companionship back in my life – someone to talk to last thing at night, someone to think about during the day – but somehow it seemed beyond my reach. I knew it was unlikely that I was going to meet anyone while I was touring. I was never in the same place for more than twenty-four hours and I wasn't the type of person to indulge in one-night stands with my fans, which, in hindsight, was probably something of a blessing since most of them were well under the age of consent.

Just as I had begun to resign myself to the fact that I wasn't going to meet anyone in the near future, the strangest thing happened – I did meet someone, and the funniest thing about it all was that she had been there, standing in front of me, all along. Her name was Danielle Gaha and she was an extremely talented singer who had been booked to tour with me for the year. Not only was she to provide superb backing vocals for the set, but it was her job to stand in for Kylie when I performed 'Especially for You'. Beautiful and gifted, it was hard not to be attracted to Danielle, and it was not long before we became involved with one another. She helped me come to terms with the demands of living on the road. And – more importantly, I felt – broadened my horizons by introducing me to Stevie Wonder, LA/Babyface, early Michael Jackson and James Taylor. Our relationship lasted for the duration of the tour, and she was my rock over that period, but when I returned to London at the end of the year we called time on our romance. We both realised that our relationship had been driven and fuelled by the shared experience of the tour, and that it probably wouldn't translate now that we were back home in the UK. And so we went our separate ways and I resigned myself to a single life again.

Chapter Thirteen

Loincloths and Luvvies

'WEBER? AS IN the barbeque manufacturer? Why would they want to work with me?'

'Jason, just how long have you lived in London now?' Richard asked. I could tell he was getting slightly exasperated with me because I could detect a faint note of sarcasm in his voice.

'I don't know, a year, maybe longer. Why?'

'I only ask because I thought by now you might realise that when people over here mention the word Webber they aren't talking about flaming bloody barbeques!'

'What?'

Richard put his head in his hands and sighed. 'I tell you what, Dono, you can take the kid out of Melbourne, but you're hard pushed to take Melbourne out of the kid!'

'What are they talking about then?'

'Not what, but who. Webber – as in Lloyd Webber – as in Andrew Lloyd Webber!'

'The name rings a bell but I just can't quite ...'

'Oh for goodness' sake, Jason – he's only the most important composer of musical theatre! *Evita, Phantom, Cats* ... Try to keep up, Dono!'

'What does he want with me?'

'He's putting on a production of *Joseph and the Amazing Technicolor Dreamcoat* and he's thinking about casting you as the lead.'

It was April 1991 and Richard I were sitting in his office in South Kensington. With everything that was going on in my career, Richard had decided to move to London permanently and had brought his wife and kids over from Australia. They were now living in a beautiful mews house (Reece Mews) off the Fulham Road, next to Francis Bacon's studio.

It had been quite a year. The tour had gone well, and although *Between the Lines* hadn't quite matched the success of *Ten Good Reasons* it had still been a hit, and we were both starting to reap the financial rewards from it all. And yet, even though my career as a pop singer was going well, Richard was starting to think ahead of the game. He realised how fickle the music industry was and knew that with the type of music I was producing, and the image I was projecting, I didn't have long in that world. My appeal lay with the teenage girl market and, as lucrative as that could be, he was only too aware of the fact that in time they would come of age and move on to something else. He didn't want me to fade out of the charts, he wanted me to capitalise on my success and use it as a bargaining tool to get me somewhere else.

I could see where he was coming from, and in truth I was getting a little jaded by the whole thing. It was all well and good being a teen pin-up, but I was growing up. I didn't want to be the squeaky-clean boy-next-door any more – for I wasn't that person in real life. I was a dope-smoking twenty-two-year-old who in his spare time liked to party. The material that Mike, Pete and Matt were giving me was great – genius even. It was hugely popular, it was failsafe, it was of its time, and the kids loved it. The only problem was that I didn't. It wasn't the type of music I listened to when I was chilling out at home in Chepstow Villas. I liked pop music, but it's fair to say that I preferred far more leftfield artists. I liked the Stones, Nirvana, Seal, Frankie Goes to Hollywood, the Happy Mondays. For some time I had thought about ways in which I could evolve my music and style to suit my own personal tastes, but when I'd put this to Richard and the guys from Stock, Aitken and Waterman they'd practically laughed me out of the office.

'If it ain't broke, kid, don't fix it,' Pete had said.

Richard had agreed. He knew that I was never going to make the transition from pop puppet to serious rock star. Even with a new look and edgier material the public wouldn't buy it.

I wasn't really convinced that a leap into musical theatre was the right move for me to make. For starters, I did wonder whether I would be able to carry it off. Although my voice was improving, the thought of standing up on stage every night and singing live was daunting to say the least. And I also wasn't sure whether I wanted my career to go in that direction. Despite what Richard and Pete had said, I was still of the view that I could make it as a credible recording artist and I didn't think a foray into theatreland would do me any favours. And, in any case, few artists in my position would have wanted to make that move, for why would you even consider the prospect of performing eight shows a week for a whole year when you could do four nights at Wembley Arena over the same period of time and earn the same amount of money – if not more.

But Richard saw things differently. Knowing that I was nearing my shelf life as a pop sensation, he wanted me to go back to my first trade – acting – and he saw a stint in a West End musical as not only the perfect bridge between the two professions but as a showcase for my talents. Dad sided with Richard. One of the highpoints of his career in the early Eighties had been his run in the Sydney Theatre Company's production of *Chicago*, and he thought it would be a chance for people to see that I was an all-rounder.

'Look, let's just go and meet Andrew and take it from there,' Richard said. 'Nothing is definite as it is. You'll have to audition for him and you may not even get the part.'

I believe I had first come to the attention of Andrew Lloyd Webber during my tour. His young daughter, Imogen, was a fan of mine and so he had – no doubt with some reluctance – taken her to see me perform in Brighton, and he had obviously liked what he'd seen, for when he decided to restage *Joseph*, the musical he had written with his then lyricist Tim Rice, he'd had me in mind from the beginning.

Andrew isn't one for wasting any time, and so after agreeing to the meeting I was soon standing in the sitting room of his elegant London home. Richard, Mike Reid and Mike Dixon, who worked with Andrew, were in the room, and the great maestro himself was at the piano.

'Okay, Jason, are you ready?'

'I guess so …'

'No need to be nervous, it's all very relaxed, very informal. Just take a deep breath and start from the top.'

I had barely got to the bottom of the page of the song sheet of 'Any Dream Will Do' when he stopped me. 'Well, I think we all know where we are at with this, don't we?' Andrew said, looking round the room. 'I think we've found our Joseph!'

I liked Andrew a lot and it quickly became apparent to me that this show wasn't some kind of end-of-the-pier panto, but a massive production at the London Palladium.

'So do you want to go with it?' Richard asked me on the way home.

'Abso-fucking-lutely! If he wants me, then I'm in!'

Later that day, Richard let Andrew know my decision. Andrew was a creative person and wasn't interested in the nuts and bolts of business, so Richard went straight to the MD of his company, Patrick McKenna, and spelled out his terms and a long list of provisos, the key one being that if I was to appear in the show then I should be allowed a profit share: for every seat in the theatre I filled I'd take a percentage home. At first Patrick was hesitant – in those days theatre work was conducted strictly on a PAYE basis – but, after a word with Andrew, he relinquished and the deal was set up.

With the ink dry on my contract, a week later I received an invitation from Andrew to join him for a weekend at his house in the country. He was excited about the show and wanted to have a creative pow-wow with Richard and myself.

I will never forget that trip to Andrew's house in Watership Down, in Hampshire, for as long as I live. Unfamiliar with that part of the country, and so fearful of getting lost, we set off in Richard's car in the early afternoon. We had taken Pete along for the ride as there was some talk about Stock, Aitken and Waterman reworking some songs on the score, which as it happened never worked out. Now, I'd seen some pretty great properties in my time, but few compared to this. I'd never seen such a long driveway in my life, and when we eventually reached the house – or, to put it more accurately, the 'pile' – we were all open-mouthed. 'It's like bloody Versailles!' Pete exclaimed.

A butler let us in and we were shown into a vast drawing room and told to wait for Andrew as he was in the middle of a call. The butler asked us whether we would like a drink and, parched from the journey, we all accepted. Still teetotal at this point in my life, I opted for a glass of water, while

Richard and Pete both had gin and tonics. It took an age for Andrew to finish his call, and by the time he arrived I think it would be fair to say that Richard and Pete were quite well-oiled, thanks to the attentiveness of the butler. Richard was quite contained, but Pete was anything but. By this stage he was so relaxed in Andrew's home that he had slunk into the sofa, and was merrily chatting away to Andrew's wife, Madeleine, who'd come to join us. To my utter horror he'd put his feet up on the table.

'I'm so sorry about that,' Andrew said as he breezed into the room. 'You must all be very thirsty – how about a trip down to the local pub?'

As we headed out to Andrew's Range Rover, I took Pete aside. 'Take it easy, mate!'

Richard, Pete and I piled into the back seat, while Andrew and Madeleine sat in the front with their Jack Russell, which they proceeded to throw out of the car every fifty yards or so for a run.

'He likes chasing rabbits,' Andrew explained. Evidently he wasn't much cop at it for after two or three moments he'd be back at the car door, with nothing to show for his efforts, wanting to get back in.

At the pub, Andrew, Richard and I talked shop, while Pete carried on chatting to Madeleine and drinking. He was getting so exuberant by this stage that I had to keep kicking him under the table. After an hour or so we left to return to the house for dinner, and on the way back the Lloyd Webbers carried on their rabbit ritual. Halfway down the drive, midway through one of the dog stops, Pete announced that he needed to pee, so he got out of the car. As he was taking his leak he noticed a dead rabbit on the ground, so he picked it up and put it in the dog's mouth. 'He's got one!' he cried. 'He's finally got one!'

The look of pride on Andrew's face was palpable, in fact had his chest puffed out any further I think he would have exploded. 'That's dinner sorted!' he said.

Andrew is a generous host and over dinner the wine flowed, and it wasn't any old wine either. Andrew wasn't the type of person to think he could get away with serving up a couple of bottles of Jacob's Creek just because we were Aussies. Oh no, it was Premier Cru from start to finish.

'This is serious stuff!' Richard said to me as he took a sip from his glass.

'You're telling me!' boomed Pete as he downed his in one.

I'm not sure how many bottles they got through that night – all I do know is that very little business was done, and in the morning both Richard and Pete were suffering.

'I tell you what,' Richard said as we got in the car to head back to London. 'I drank so much bloody claret that when I woke up this morning and looked in the mirror my teeth were black!'

All Pete could manage was a groan. 'I swear I'm never going to touch another drop in my life ...'

'Yeah, right!' I said.

* * *

I think I could be forgiven for feeling a little nervous as I walked into the studio in Battersea on the first day of rehearsals. As I opened the door and saw fifty or so faces turn towards me I couldn't help but feel like an impostor. Everyone in that room, be they cast or production crew, director or pianist, was a professional. They had spent their lives treading the boards in theatre, doing their time, and it meant everything to them. And then there was me, some guy off *Top of the Pops*, who didn't have a single second of stage experience to my name, and I was about to give them their lead in this production.

Even though it was our first read-through everyone's delivery was so pitch-perfect it was frightening. I could feel the pressure, their eyes on me every time it came to my turn, and when I had to sing for the first time sweat poured from my brow and I felt my cheeks burn up. But somehow I got through it, and when the day came to an end I'd even managed to get a couple of pats on the back. However, despite their kind words of praise and encouragement, I kept feeling like a complete and utter charlatan on my journey home, and I realised that this was beginning to be something of the story of my life. With every job I walked into I felt like a fraud, whether it was on my first few days on *Neighbours* or at the beginning of my music career.

'But you managed to make a success of both of those,' Dad said when I rang him that night.

'Yes, but this time it's different. I'm out there on my own.'

'Look, Jason, you really have to learn to have some faith in yourself. Do you really think that Andrew Lloyd Webber would have come to you if he thought you couldn't cut it? He's got as much to lose as you do, more so even, if this doesn't work out. You've got one of the greatest impresarios in the world thinking you can do it. That means something in itself.'

I understood what Dad was saying and his encouragement helped, but I also realised that having faith in myself wasn't enough. If I was going to pull this off I was going to have to work really hard at it, to give it my complete all. I didn't want to let anyone down, whether it was Andrew, the director Stephen Pimlott, the choreographer Anthony van Laast, the cast and crew, or the public who'd be paying good money to see the show. I'd always been pretty dedicated when it came to work, but I knew that this time I was going to have to go that extra mile, for I didn't have any of the safety nets I'd had in the past. There was no editing process in this game, no technician on hand to iron out any problems with my voice, no chance of another take were I to fluff my lines. This was it, the real deal. I was going live. And as much as I knew that when you worked in theatre you were very much part of a company, no matter what your role was, I was also acutely aware that this show was being sold on my name. I felt a deep sense of responsibility to get it right, because if I didn't the whole show would suffer.

With that in mind I took singing lessons with Ian Adam, the vocal coach who'd trained Michael Crawford. I spent hours at night poring over my scripts and learning the choreography of the stage directions. I stopped smoking weed because I knew that it was bad for my voice, and spent hours at the gym so that I would be physically fit for the show. My commitment to the production bordered on fanaticism, but that was okay with me for I knew that it would pay off in the end.

The day we took the rehearsals for the show out of the studio and into the Palladium was a memorable one for me. As I stood on the stage for the first time that morning and looked out into the empty auditorium, taking in the surroundings of the old Edwardian music hall, I guess it dawned on me for the first time that this was really happening. In a couple of weeks those red velvet seats would be starting to fill, the orchestra would be warming up, I would be waiting in the wings, and as soon as the lights went down, the show would begin. It was quite an alarming prospect, but there was no turning back at this point, for as I made my way to the theatre in Argyll Street that day they were already putting the hoardings up. *Joseph and the Amazing Technicolor Dreamcoat starring JASON DONO-VAN. Book Now to Avoid Disappointment!*

That afternoon we gathered in the bar of the Palladium and went through our Sitzprobe, the moment in a musical production where the orchestra and vocalists run through the score for the first time together, and I have to say that, as apprehensive as I had been about it the night before, it was one of the most exhilarating experiences of my working life. For months I had worked with just piano accompaniment, but hearing my voice now, against a full-blown orchestra, I suddenly felt like a musical singer.

From the outset Andrew had wanted this production of *Joseph* to be the biggest, flashest, most impressive one he had ever staged, and no expense had been spared. He had called upon the services of Mark Thompson, one of the leading theatre designers of his generation. There were sets that took you straight back to those Canaan Days, and a choir of children so large I wondered whether they would even fit on stage. There were camels and sheep, an army of hairdressers and make-up artists, a resident wig-maker, revolves, hydraulics, not to mention some back-line alcoholics: this show was to be massive. The aim was not to rival any of the productions currently shown on the West End, but to eclipse them.

Mark was also responsible for the costumes. I guess most people would assume that working as a costume designer on *Joseph* must be a pretty straightforward task. I mean, once you've got that multicoloured coat worked out the job is pretty much done. But Mark wasn't like that, his attention to detail was quite extraordinary, and he had an eye for perfection. He and I worked very closely together initially. As much as he wanted me to 'be' Joseph, he also wanted to bring some of my own personality into the look. So as well as Joseph's coat and the god-awful loincloth he wore, Mark gave him baggy socks as a sort of nod to the skateboard look Scott had been so famous for. And there wasn't just

one Dreamcoat either, but three: the original velvet one
Joseph is given by his father (which, rather naughtily, is still
in my possession), a tattered one for the scene in which his
brothers shred it, and one that was pieced together with
Velcro so that it could be ripped off. It was also decided, for
a reason that I could never quite understand, that Joseph
should have a mullet of long blond hair, so a wig was made
for me. I hated that wig more than anything, for not only
did I feel stupid in it but it was so bloody uncomfortable to
wear. It was really hot under there and it made my head
itch, but the worst thing about it was that it was very tight,
and literally had to be yanked off me at the end of the night.
Now, my mother's father was as bald as a badger, so I was
always destined to be follically challenged but I had assumed
that it would come to me in old age, not when I was twenty-
two, and having that thing ripped off me every evening was
not only painful but resulted in me losing a lot of hair in the
process. As my hair came out I became conscious of the fact
that I was looking less and less like my waxwork in Rock
Circus, and that had a profound effect on my psyche.

With every costume fitting, run-through on the stage,
practice with the hydraulics and lighting check, the show
became less of a concept and more of a reality to me. I *was*
Joseph. It hadn't been a long journey but it was a pretty
intense one, and at last I was there.

'You're going to be brilliant!' Andrew said as he popped
his head round my dressing-room door on opening night.
I had just got into costume and was sitting in my chair

waiting for the final touches to be made to my make-up. Through the Tannoy system I could hear the orchestra warming up and the auditorium starting to fill.

'Half an hour till curtain call, Mr Donovan,' came the announcement.

We were expecting a full house that night – and every other night, it seemed, for the next twelve months from when the box office first opened was an instant sell-out.

It was all very well for Andrew to feel confident. He'd been doing this kind of thing all his life – indeed, according to legend he'd written his first piece of music at the age of five, and by all accounts it wasn't that bad. But for me it was a whole different story. I was putting myself on the line here, going for a wave that I wasn't sure I was good enough to catch, taking the drop. I know that a lot of people had been sceptical about whether I could do it too. There had been a little bit of sniping going around – not in the theatre itself, but around town and in the press. I didn't blame them – I felt the same way myself at times, and I could see where they were coming from. Back in the early Nineties there wasn't such a thing as celebrity theatre. You didn't have your TV presenters and weather girls kicking their heels in *Chicago*, or models mouthing off about men in *The Vagina Monologues*, and so forth. If a soap star wanted to tread the boards, then you took yourself off to do panto in Wimbledon. You certainly didn't have the audacity to dare to show up in the West End and expect people to come to see you.

With ten minutes to go before show-time, I slowly made my way to the wings, stage left. 'You can do this, you can do this,' I kept telling myself. I carefully stepped onto the hydraulic rise, focused on my diaphragm and my breathing, centred my thoughts on the task ahead – and with that the curtain went up and I absolutely fucking shat myself!

Chapter Fourteen

Face Up

WHEN THE CURTAIN came down on the show that night I knew that I had pulled it off, for the audience broke into a thunderous applause, and when I returned to the stage to take my bow, to my amazement, the entire house, led by my father who had flown out for the occasion, rose to their feet and gave me a standing ovation.

'It was a triumph, an absolute triumph!' Andrew exclaimed at the opening-night party at the Natural History Museum. 'The audience just loved it! They simply couldn't get enough of it. It's a guaranteed hit, you'll see.'

And it was. Almost without exception, the critics lauded it as a 'triumph' and heralded me as the new star of the West End. Even those who'd been sceptical about my casting were forced to eat humble pie, for they could find little fault in my performance. With such favourable reviews, overnight *Joseph* became a 'must see' production and celebrities flocked to the Palladium in their droves. The Princess of Wales brought William and Harry along for a holiday treat, and they came and introduced themselves afterwards, which was something of an honour. Ben Elton saw the show and subsequently sent me a letter of congratulations. Stephen Fry attended, as did the Pet Shop Boys, Liza Minnelli, Elton John and Shirley Bassey, who all took their seats among the general public for the Technicolor experience. Even Kylie came.

I was thrilled that I had been able to pull it off and do justice to the role, but I didn't have much time to bask in my glory, for as Dad (who'd spent most of the night marvelling in the fact that there was an Australian theme to the after-show party) pointed out, the following day I'd have to be up there doing it all again – and again, and again. I was appearing in eight shows a week, with only my Sundays free, and I had signed up to this for a year. But, as gruelling as my schedule was, I wasn't in a position to complain. Thanks to Richard's ruthless negotiations and his insistence that I should receive a profit-share in the show, as it was a total sell-out I was taking home over £30,000 a week. I had never earned so much money in my life.

And yet, the funny thing was that the money didn't mean that much to me. I didn't have the time or the inclination to go wild with it, or, as we say in Australia, spunk my cash. I was happy with my lot. I had a nice flat, I'd bought a car (a racing-green Range Rover, which I loved), but at the end of

the day I was happiest cycling around town on my push-
bike.

I have always held the view that no matter how far your
star rises in life you should always keep it real. Don't believe
the hype, be true to the person you were before all the
madness started, keep your feet firmly on the ground and
that way you'll remain both happy and sane. As far as the
audience and the critics were concerned I may have been the
star of the show, but I didn't see it that way. I was just part of
a very large team. The fact that my name happened to headline the billing was irrelevant to me, for the way I saw it my
contribution to the show was just as valuable as anyone
else's. I wasn't going to start swanning in and out of the
theatre like some kind of diva, treating the rest of the
company as though they were inferior to me, that simply
wasn't my style. In any case, over the two or three months
we had been working together these people had become my
friends – Megan, Lindsey, Johnny and Nadia, to name a few.
On matinee days when the weather was good I'd while away
the break in between performances with a gang of guys from
the back line on the theatre roof. It was a hot summer that
year and it was good to feel the rays on our back. From time
to time I'd sit with them as they got stuck into the beers and
went for their fag breaks. On rainy days we'd congregate in
my dressing room, muck about behind the sets, and on a
Friday night I would take them to Lawrence's pad in Soho to
party. There was a very friendly atmosphere among the cast
and crew on that production and we had some really

wonderful times together. So as far as I was concerned we were a happy ship, but what I didn't see at the time is that we were fast sailing into uncharted waters.

It was the back-line guys who first alerted me to the posters. I'm not sure why I hadn't noticed them myself, for they'd been dotted around the area surrounding the theatre for some time. I guess I was always in such a hurry to get into the building, trying not to get too waylaid by the group of fans who patiently congregated by the back door each day, so I never had the chance to clock them. But, sure enough, they were there for everyone to see.

I remember posing for the photograph in the poster. It had been taken by Channel Ten's in-house photographer, Dennis, up in Nunawading for a charity event when I was still in *Neighbours*, and there had been a lot of talk on the morning of the shoot as to what I should wear. In the end I decided to keep it simple and opted for jeans and a plain white T-shirt. But in this reproduction of that photograph my T-shirt was no longer plain white, for the slogan 'Queer as Fuck' had been superimposed across it. My name was printed at the top of the poster, and at the bottom was the word 'OUT'.

I wasn't sure how to react when I saw the poster properly for the first time. There was part of me that wanted to see the funny side of it because it was so outrageous, but when it was explained to me that this wasn't just some practical joke being played on me by a member of the crew, and that I'd become the target of an 'outing' campaign, my humour faded pretty fast.

The practice of outing first began at the start of the 1990s in the US, when a group of militant gay activists launched a campaign in which they sought to expose those in the public eye whom they believed to be closeting their sexuality, be they politicians or Hollywood stars. Jodie Foster, Tom Selleck, Whitney Houston, John Travolta, the music mogul David Geffen and the gossip columnist Liz Smith were just some of the names who'd been targeted when the campaign kicked off. If the 'outers' had even the slightest misplaced suspicion that you were gay and were covering it up, then that was it: bang, your face was up on a poster, named and shamed with the words 'Absolutely Queer' under your mug-shot, and, depending on your sex, 'fag' or 'dyke' attached to your name. Your crime wasn't that you were gay, it was that you were lying about being gay, and as such were not only a hypocrite but were guilty of undermining the rights and causes of your community.

The campaign caused a huge amount of controversy at the time, not least within the gay community itself, which was deeply divided on the issue. Its defenders viewed it as a moral war on hypocrisy; while its critics believed it to be a vindictive, aggressive campaign, one that violated a person's human right to privacy, and the fact that these allegations were often based on nothing more than hearsay made it all the more hateful in their eyes.

I had always known where I stood on the debate, for I have always maintained that everyone is entitled to a private life, but now that I was a victim of this campaign I held those views with an even stronger sense of conviction. And yet it could be argued that my principles had boomeranged on me, for had I not gone out of my way to deny my relationship with Kylie, and if we had just come clean about it right from the start, then maybe, just maybe, I wouldn't have been in the position I now found myself in.

I had known for some time that there were rumours doing the rounds about me being gay, and I was completely fine with that. You can't work in the industry I do and worry about such things. In both my incarnations as a soap and pop star I was always the pretty boy, never the hard man. I was Jason Donovan, not Russell Crowe. And the world of musical theatre isn't exactly the most macho of professions, so it's easy to see why people thought I might be friends with Dorothy. I mean, let's face it, I was getting up on stage every night in a long blond wig, a face full of make-up and wearing nothing more than a loincloth, singing, '*I look handsome, I look smart, I am a walking work of art* ...' Is it any wonder that people were talking?

Having people think I was gay wasn't a problem to me because I didn't see it as an insult; it was just something that was incorrect. It's as simple as that. I know who I have been to bed with in my life, and I can honestly say, hand on heart, that none of them were men. That doesn't make me homophobic, it means that I'm a heterosexual and as such I like women, or, to be more precise, *love* women.

I'd always been pretty straight up about this with the press. If I was asked whether I was gay or not, I would say no, I wasn't, but I was always careful not to go any further for I really valued my privacy. I'd had girlfriends since Kylie but I always felt very ungallant about discussing them in the press. I had just started seeing a girl called Tara Owens at around this time, and although she was a model she valued her privacy. It was the early days of our relationship, and while I didn't keep the fact that I was seeing her a secret, I didn't advertise it either.

I was perfectly willing to accept the whispers about my sexuality, but when I saw the posters it was another story – this was hardcore, and there was no escape from it for they had been strategically placed around the West End. They were in Argyll Street and Regent Street, up in Piccadilly, and dotted around the Tottenham Court Road. So I may have missed them as I cycled into work and hurried into the theatre each day, but what about the commuter standing at the bus stop in the evening, or the shop girls taking their lunch breaks on Carnaby Street, or the man making his way to work on the tube? They had time to take them in.

I realised there was little I could do about it. Fearful of being sued, the group responsible for the campaign in the UK operated underground, and no one seemed to know who they were. My only recourse, with the help of my friends in the crew, was to pull them down one by one. I hoped and prayed that it would all just die down, that eventually the posters would stop appearing, but if anything the campaign just gained more momentum. Then, in the summer of 1991, a journalist from the magazine *The Face* decided to follow up on the story.

Established in the early Eighties, *The Face* was the style bible for the young. If you wanted to be hip and cool, learn about the latest fads and trends before anyone else did and get in touch with street culture, then this was the magazine for you. Unlike the other mainstream publications on the stands at the time, *The Face* didn't follow fashion, it dictated it. This was the magazine that declared Madonna a cultural icon, had us wearing Doc Martens with kilts, and launched the careers of a long list of designers, photographers and writers who might have never made it onto the radar had they not been discovered by the publication. John Richmond, Juergen Teller and Julie Burchill were just a few names who showcased their talent within its pages, but perhaps the greatest star they launched in their time was a little-known teenage model from Croydon. Her name was Kate Moss, and those first pictures of her wearing nothing more than a feather headdress, taken by Corinne Day, would propel her into superstardom overnight.

The Face had been founded by a guy called Nick Logan, and it was run out of his publishing house Wagadon. Nick had been an editor at *NME* and had also been responsible for the launch of *Smash Hits*, a teenage music magazine that I regularly featured in.

I'd always been a great admirer of *The Face*, and when I first moved to the UK I was a regular reader. I liked the design, I liked the photographs, and it was a good read. As much as I couldn't complain about being a *Smash Hits* cover boy, there were moments when I did wonder whether I could achieve the kind of kudos that might take me into *The Face* instead, but I knew that for as long as I continued to produce my particular brand of pop that was never going to happen.

It was easy to see why *The Face* wanted to follow up the 'outing' story. While outing had been going on in the US for nearly a year, the practice had only just hit these shores, so it was an interesting subject for them to tackle, and they knew that it was one that would be popular with their readers. Although I was by no means the only target in the UK campaign, I had been the first, and so it was also quite understandable that they would use me as the peg of their article.

When Richard initially told me on the telephone about the piece I thought that I didn't have anything to worry about. I was convinced that they would handle the subject fairly – perhaps, given their usual stance on things, they might even condemn the practice. The article, which was in their August issue, had been commissioned by the magazine's editor, Sheryl Garratt, and was written by a journalist called Ben Summerskill.

However, 'I think you'd better come over and have a look at it, Jase,' Richard said to me. 'It's not great, in fact I think it could be libellous.'

I was shocked when I read the article for the first time. This wasn't the balanced piece I had been expecting, it was anything but. To illustrate the article they had chosen the image taken from the posters of me in the 'Queer as Fuck' T-shirt, used a full-blown version of it and failed to mention anywhere in the copy that this had been doctored by the activists. The article was a straightforward piece of reportage on the movement and at the beginning of the piece it did concede that I had been its 'luckless first victim', but it didn't make it clear anywhere in the text that I wasn't gay – and by this omission, and the general tenor of the piece, the inference was that the 'boy with the bleached hair', as they dubbed me, was in fact a liar. They had gone so far as to use a quote from an earlier article in which I had said I wasn't gay, but if anything this just made things worse, for it looked like I was in denial.

I was horrified.

'What do you think I should do?' I asked.

'I'm not sure,' Richard said. 'I mean, it's pretty much saying that you are gay.'

'I don't care about that, Richard, what I care about is the fact they're inferring that I'm covering it up and lying about it! That's what pisses me off. It's one thing when it's on the posters, but when it's in a magazine – a magazine like this that *everyone* reads – that's bad. I don't want people who read this to think I'm an out-and-out liar. Why didn't they approach me about this first? I could and would have set the record straight.'

'Look, anyone who knows you realises that isn't the case ...'

'Yes, but what about the people that don't know me! It's here in print. They are going to think it's true.'

Richard paused for a moment. 'I know, it's not good, it's not good at all.'

'So what am I going to do?'

'I think we should go back to the magazine, state our case and get an apology.'

'Do you think that will work?'

'I can't see why not. The fact is, there is no truth to what they are saying about you whatsoever. If we make that clear to them, then they will have to concede. They can't go printing stuff that isn't true, they're a reputable magazine after all. Look, leave it with me, I'll deal with it.'

I think Richard assumed that he'd be able to sort everything out quite quickly. He'd put in a call to Nick Logan, explain the situation, and once Nick realised the truth he'd run an apology, maybe in the form of an interview, or perhaps as an article in which I could give my side of the story. But that wasn't to happen. Instead, Nick stood steadfastly by the story, and refused to see it from my point of view.

'I think we are going to have to seek legal advice on this,' Richard said to me the following week.

'Are you sure?'

'Look, one stiff letter and they'll come round.'

I told Richard to go ahead as I was becoming increasingly distressed about it all. The story had been followed up in Australia and both Mum and Dad had been doorstepped by the press, who wanted to know more. 'Why is your son in such denial about his sexuality, Terry? Is it because he is trying to protect his career and doesn't want to alienate his female fans? What kind of message is that sending out?' When Mum called to tell me what had happened she was in tears.

That week my solicitors at Sheridan's wrote to Nick Logan and stated my case, notifying them that there was simply no truth to their suggestion that I was a hypocrite or a liar when it came to my sexuality. They pointed out that at no stage in the run-up to the publication of the article had the journalist contacted me to substantiate the claim or ask me what my reaction to it was. As such, they demanded an apology.

Four days later we got a response, but to my astonishment there was not a single word of apology or retraction. They were standing their ground.

'How would you like to proceed from here, Jason?' my solicitor, Howard Jones, asked.

'I don't know ... I've never been in this position before.'

'Well, you have grounds for a case, and if you want to vindicate your reputation then you could start legal proceedings.'

'Take them to court?'

'Not necessarily. If you instigate proceedings they might realise that you are taking this seriously and they might come round. No one ever wants to end up in court, and I'm sure some kind of settlement could be reached.'

I turned to Richard. 'What do you think?'

'I think we should go for it. I can't see we have any other choice. Sometimes you have to play hardball.'

I have no regrets in my life (life is too short); but if there is one moment I'm not particularly proud of, it is taking *The Face* to court. I still stand by the view that I was right and they were wrong, but with hindsight I would have done things differently, for I had no idea of just what I was letting myself in for. I was only twenty-three at the time, and although I may have thought I was a man, in some ways I was still incredibly green around the ears. I didn't see the wider picture, I didn't understand the ramifications of it all. I simply thought I was doing the right thing.

To be fair, I guess we all thought that *The Face* would apologise, and none of us wanted it to go to trial. It wasn't my intention to drag the magazine or Nick, who was ill with cancer at the time, through the courts. I was of the genuine belief that they would say sorry and all this could then have been put behind us once and for all. But to everyone's amazement, in the months that led up to the case they refused to be moved. At the eleventh hour they tried to make throughways and sent letters to me, but it was too little too late, for there was still no apology, and so we had no other choice but to take it to trial.

The libel case was held at Court Thirteen of the High Court and lasted for five days. On the day I was due to testify I had to skip a matinee performance of *Joseph* and I remember that well, for it was the first performance of the show I had missed since the run began. As it was I wasn't nervous about testifying. This wasn't something that I had to rehearse. When you stand up and tell the truth, these aren't lines you have to learn, for they are words that come from the heart.

I stood there in the witness box and in a steady voice I told it as it was. When questioned by both the defence and the prosecution I told the court that I didn't think my alleged homosexuality was a slur on my name, but what I wholeheartedly objected to was the implication that I had lied about my sexuality, and I felt that this was incredibly damaging in both a personal and professional capacity.

'In my position, particularly with young kids and certainly with *Joseph*, people look to me as an influence on young people. I think I would see myself as a role model.'

The jury agreed and I won my case. The judge awarded me £200,000 in damages and a further £100,000 in costs. But that was irrelevant to me. I hadn't gone to court to make money; I had done it to clear my name.

When I walked out of the front door of the courtroom there was a media scrum. 'Are you relieved to have cleared your name, Jason?' 'What are you going to do with the money?' 'How does it feel?'

How did it feel? Well, of course I was glad to have won, to have proved my point, to have cleared my name, but as I made my way down the steps of the High Court I couldn't help but feel that there was something bittersweet about this victory.

'Oy! You! You're that Jason Donovan, aren't you?' a cab driver shouted at me. 'Lend us a tenner!'

Chapter Fifteen

Close Every Door to Me

THERE HAD BEEN a lot of media interest in the libel trial right from the start, and so when the judge's verdict came through in April 1992 it was headline news both in the UK and abroad. It was one of the lead items on both the BBC and ITV television news that night, and the next day it made the front pages of both the tabloids and broadsheets alike. It was followed up in Europe and Asia, where I still enjoyed strong fan bases, and back at home it was the breaking story of the morning. On the ABC network it fell to my mother to report the news, for by chance she happened to be working that day, which was slightly surreal for us both.

That night my telephone rang off the hook as calls from family, friends and colleagues came in. They were offering me their congratulations, which was kind of them, but to be really honest I wasn't in the mood for their warm words.

The fact was that I didn't feel I had anything to celebrate. Yes, I had won. I had been vindicated in the eyes of the law, but for me it was a hollow victory. I had never wanted things to go that far as it was; all I had ever set out to do was to get an apology from the magazine, a public acknowledgement that I was neither a liar nor a hypocrite. It had never been my intention to have my day in court.

The run-up to the trial had been an extremely difficult time for me. They were dark days, and as much as Richard and my legal team were on hand to support me, I couldn't help but feel that I was out there on my own. There were times when I thought I just couldn't cope with it all. I'd had my fair share of troubles in the past, moments of self-doubt, worry, heartache and pain, but all that had been just part of my rites of passage, no different from the experiences of many boys my age. But what separated me from my peers was the world I was moving in. Though they had troubles of their own, none of my friends had to contend with what I was going through. The pressure of the trial, the endless meetings with my solicitors and my QC, the testimonies, the written evidence, the sworn affidavits – it was all quite alien to me, and as such quite daunting. At times I felt it was all beyond my grasp.

At night I would get up on stage, do my song and dance routine and be all smiles for the audience, for I was professional enough to know that the show had to go on, but when I walked off stage and out of the spotlight I lived under a heavy cloud.

'Hey, Jase, want to come up to the roof for a while and chill out with us?' the crew would ask.

'Not today,' I would say, trying to sound as cheery as possible. 'I've got to get home. Stuff to do and all that, but I'll see you tomorrow.'

'Okay. Take it easy, mate!'

On the night of the verdict, before I went to bed I rolled myself a big fat joint and sat there alone in my flat contemplating everything that had happened. My lawyers had been delighted by the result and Richard had been happy too, but it was easier for them. To them it was all about winning, and they had achieved that, they'd got the result they wanted. After the verdict they'd gone back to Sheridans and got stuck into a bottle of champagne. That pop of the cork served as a full stop, marking the end of a difficult chapter in all their lives, but for me it was different. I had enough foresight to see that this wasn't the end, it was just the beginning, and as I lay back on my sofa and smoked the rest of the joint dry I was overwhelmed with a deep sense of foreboding. I knew there and then that I had scored an own goal.

By taking on *The Face* all I had ever set out to do was to restore my reputation and stand up for myself, and at the time I believed that was the right thing to do, but in the days that followed the verdict it quickly became clear that I had made the biggest mistake of my life and had completely misjudged the situation. What I hadn't realised at the time was that by suing *The Face* and winning I had effectively waged war on a British institution, and no one liked that: I might as well have given the Queen Mother a good slap around the gills for all the ensuing backlash I got. Overnight, I went from being the toast of the town to the most vilified person in London.

The reason for such a public uproar was that during the case Nick Logan had claimed that, should the magazine lose, there was a likelihood that he would have to fold *The Face*, as they simply couldn't afford to pay any damages or my costs on top of their own legal bill.

Now, from the outset, when it became apparent that we were going to have to go to trial, my lawyers had sat me down and gone through all the various outcomes that could arise from the verdict, and I'd decided there and then that if I was to win I would return the majority of any damages back to the magazine. It had never been my intention to profit from the case, and even when those around me huffed and puffed about the damage this was doing to my career and how I was entitled to remuneration for any money lost down the line, I still wasn't interested. I was never in this for financial gain, it had always been a matter of principle.

Because *The Face* had got me into this position in the first place, I thought it was only fair that they should pay my legal costs, but as far as I was concerned they could take what money they wanted and needed from the rest of the pot. It was there on the table, and I made this clear to them shortly after the trial drew to a close. In many respects it was generous of me, for what few people realised at the time was that *The Face* was not the independent, homespun magazine Nick was leading everyone to believe it was. Although it had started in the Eighties as a one-man band, towards the end of the decade the publishing giant Condé Nast had acquired a forty per cent stake in it, and as such there was money in the background – i.e. there was a safety net. Had they not had this backup then I wouldn't have sued them, but I knew that they were never going to be left high and dry, and that *The Face* was not going to fold because of me. I knew that; my lawyers knew that; Nick knew that. The only problem was that no one else seemed to.

Before I even had the chance to open my chequebook the tin started rattling. In the May issue of the magazine, Nick and his team launched an appeal to 'Save the Face'. It was named the Lemon Fund, a snide reference to a revelation in court that I used lemon juice to lighten my hair. While Nick acknowledged in his editorial note that I had agreed to spread the costs of my lawyers' bills over an eighteen-month period, he refrained to mention that I had offered further financial support. Instead he pleaded with his readers to get on board and pledge support for the magazine by either sending contributions to the offices in Pine Street or by getting involved in fundraising activities such as club nights.

Within days the pledges came flooding through. The faxes at their offices whirred, phones rang, and cheques came in by the sack-load. Around the clubs in London, places that I often frequented, buckets were passed round;

and Oliver Peyton, a leading figure in the London restaurant and club scene, staged a benefit night at his club, Raw.

I was mortified.

'It's really not that bad, Dono,' Richard said. 'In a couple of weeks it'll all die down and be forgotten about. Ultimately, you've done the right thing, and in the end you'll gain respect for standing up for yourself.'

But it didn't die down, if anything it just got worse. I was turned away from a nightclub with a bunch of friends on the grounds that I was not welcome in their establishment any more. I was asked to leave a clothes shop, sworn and spat at in the street, and had my car kicked in, which were very unpleasant experiences.

I found it all very hard to cope with. I didn't want people to resent or despise me. By nature I was a very sociable person: I liked people, and I wanted them to like me back. I was always eager to please. I didn't like fallouts, I hated confrontation of any kind. I didn't even like arguing. And yet here I was, the social pariah of London, the person it seemed that everyone wanted to hate. It was a strange position to find myself in.

Of course, the great irony of all this was that by trying to stand up for my reputation I had effectively ruined it. I had shot myself in the foot, and it hurt – it really, really hurt. Maybe it would have been better to be seen as a liar and a hypocrite after all, rather than the man who'd tried to bring down *The Face*.

I did a lot of thinking over that time, and a lot of growing up as a result. To date, my life had been just one merry skip down the Yellow Brick Road, but now I was walking on the dark side. The aftershock of the trial and the subsequent public backlash towards me made me question my identity and take a look at my life as a whole.

Aside from what had happened with the trial, on the face of it I had it all and so had very little to complain about. *Joseph* was going well, my own records were selling, and I had released a couple of singles and an album on the back of the show that had done extremely well. I had more money in the bank than I needed, a beautiful flat in London, and property back home in Australia. I mean, hey, it wasn't a bad life – on the face of it.

There was no question that prior to the trial I had been riding on the crest of a wave; and yet, while that was all very well and good I couldn't see where it was going to take me. Where did I go from here? I'd tried to evolve as a pop act, and in 1991 had taken the decision to leave Stock, Aitken and Waterman and sign with Polydor. As much as I liked Pete, Mike and Matt on a personal level, I felt very constrained working under the umbrella of their company, for it was very restrictive. I wanted to have more control of my career and reach another level with my music, but I felt that the management were holding me back.

However, the move to Polydor was not a success, and for some reason I lost my direction along the way. At the end of the day the album just didn't come together, and despite hiring some of the best producers around it was, frankly, all over the place. One of the problems I had back then was that I had spent too long on stage. I'd suddenly got all musical theatre, a little bit 'Ta Na!', and I had lost the edge on my pop voice. And the album we were working on didn't seem to be coming together, there was no sense of cohesion to it. Without enough good new material the record company were keen to capitalise on my former success, and were trying to persuade me to bolster the album with some of my old hits and a couple of *Joseph* tunes, which really depressed me. In my eyes I had failed. I'd wanted to produce something I was proud of, something with character, that reflected a more mature and edgy Jason Donovan, but I hadn't been able to turn it around. In the industry's eyes, I hadn't delivered. It was incredibly frustrating.

I so desperately wanted to develop as an act. I wanted people to see the real me, as opposed to the manufactured version of myself that was being put out there by the music industry. I wanted to leap from the cover of *Smash Hits* into the pages of *The Face*, but, of course, that was never going to happen now, and that realisation just compounded my feelings of frustration, disillusionment and despair.

There were times when I felt my life was suspended in amber. In the public consciousness I would forever be the boy-next-door, the teen heart-throb, the squeaky-clean idol, and that had been great and wonderful while I was that person. But I wasn't a teenage boy any more, I was a twenty-three-year-old man now, and I wasn't just growing up, I was growing older, something that struck me every time I looked in my dressing-room mirror and examined my thinning hair. How long could I keep the charade up? How long did I want to keep it going? For all his millions, his fans and his good deeds, the fact was I didn't want to become the new Cliff Richard, god bless him. I didn't want to be the boy that never grew up, to morph into some kind of Peter Pan Man. I simply wanted to be myself.

I felt quite alone that summer, and for the first time since I'd made that initial move to London I suffered from home-sickness. I longed to be back in Melbourne surrounded by my family and old friends, people who wouldn't judge me, who understood me, who liked and loved me for who I was. I wanted to be back in the living room in Union Street listening to Dad spouting off his wisdom as he sat on the sofa, beer in hand. I needed the warmth, love and sense of security that only Gran seemed to be able to offer me. I wanted to see Marlene and talk through the night with her like we used to. To my abject sadness, she and Dad had split up two years earlier, but we'd vowed to each other that we would always be close, and that their divorce wouldn't affect our relationship.

'I think it's gone a little too far for that to happen, don't you, Jase? I'll always be there for you, no matter what's gone on between your father and me. There may not be any blood between us, but in my mind you'll always be one of my own,' she had said to me.

As it was, she had only moved round the corner, for despite their differences she and Dad were determined to remain close for Paul's sake.

And I really missed James. I had a great network of friends in London – including Richard, Lawrence, and the photographer Peter Mac – but as much as I loved them all and as hugely supportive to me as they were at that time, I knew that James was the one person I could turn to at moments like this. No words would be said, for that wasn't how we were with one another. We'd just get in the car, head out to the beach, light a big fat Scooby-Doo, take a couple of tokes, put on our wetties and run out to the sea to catch that wave. As I have always maintained, who needs therapy when you've got the sea? The salt on your face, the offshore breeze, the rush of the wave, that's what you need when you're in trouble.

But I wasn't in a position where I could just up-sticks and leave London. Although I knew that Andrew would have given me time off if I asked, I felt I had to stay. Tickets had been sold on the back of my name, and I was damned if I was going to let people down, especially not the ones who were still on my side.

I was confused about so many things in my life during that time that, had I been a drinker, I'm sure I would have hit the bottle, but as it was I found my solace elsewhere. Back then, smoking spliffs seemed to be the only way I could escape the nightmare of what was going on in my life. With a joint in my hand I could put everything behind me.

It gave me a sense of release; it calmed me down; it took the edge off my worries and woes. I'd always liked to have a couple of puffs of spliff when I came back at night after a performance, for I needed to unwind before I went to bed, but I was restrained in my intake. I knew that smoking wasn't good for the vocal cords and I didn't want to feel too groggy in the morning, especially if I had a matinee performance that day.

But by the summer of 1992 I had taken my drug habit to another level, for that was the time when I discovered cocaine. And oblivion seemed the only way forward.

Chapter Sixteen

Bottom Line

WHY DID I take drugs? I took them because I enjoyed taking them, that's why. I liked the way they made me feel. I liked what they did for me. I liked who I was when I was on them. Whether I was stoned from smoking grass or high from taking cocaine, I enjoyed being out of it. It was as simple as that. When, at the height of my habit, I stupidly spouted this line to a reporter in an interview it became headline news, but even then I didn't care, for the way I saw it I was simply telling the truth.

Back then I never regarded drugs to be the social evil the media was purporting them to be. I could only see the positive in them because they made me feel pretty damn good. For me, getting a high was a way of escape, a form of self-expression. When I was smoking dope I found the world to be a richer place, full of life, texture and colour, as though I was looking through the filter of a lens or at a Sidney Nolan painting. When I was using cocaine, at once everything became that much more exhilarating. After a couple of lines of coke I felt like I was invincible, that I could conquer the world. It boosted my confidence, filled me with energy, gave me the kick I felt I needed.

From my early teens, when I had earned the name Bongo-van thanks to the time and effort I spent on constructing our bongs, I'd got a taste for the big hit. Sitting over that Spring Valley bottle, with its rubber piping and its steel stem that I'd sought out from a Melbourne shop that specialised in drug paraphernalia, I couldn't help but feel a sense of anticipation as the fume from the burning grass filled the vessel and I got myself into position for my draw. I liked getting high.

I could never see the point of alcohol. It wasn't the taste that put me off, it was what it did to people – all it ever seemed to do was mess them up. As a child I had hated it when Dad had a few too many, for in my mind he went from Jekyll to Hyde. Then, in my teens, when friends started experimenting with booze – apple cider and stubbies of beer – they would invariably end up stumbling around, falling over themselves, throwing up over flowerbeds and girls. I just couldn't see the appeal, it just seemed so ugly to me. I was far happier hanging out at my favourite breaks, such as Winki Pop, Jan Juc or Bells Beach, with a joint in hand. I'd sit on the beach, listening to Midnight Oil on my Walkman, marvelling in the kaleidoscope of colours that lay before me as I traced pictures into the sand or stared out to sea watching the lines of the swell. Even when I'd come to London and made it in the music industry, where there was a never-ending flow of champagne, I still wasn't tempted. 'A glass of Moët, Jason?' 'A drop of Bolly?' I'd politely turn down each glass that came my way and ask for a soft drink instead. Unlike dope, or coke even, in my mind alcohol did nothing for the senses, all it did was numb and blur them. It made people aggressive, argumentative, maudlin and ultimately quite tiresome and, the way I saw it, totally full of shit. I didn't understand what pleasure could be derived from being drunk. I've always thought that if you were a policeman and had the choice of breaking up two parties, one full of drunks and the other full of potheads, then I know which one I would choose.

If I was going to get out of it I wanted a drug that made me happy and full of life – for me that was the bottom line. I wanted to feel good about myself and life in general. I wanted to laugh, to dance, to talk, to feel and be creative, and as far as I was concerned that's how I was when I was smoking dope or using cocaine.

I must have been around eighteen years old when I first came into contact with coke. I was on one of my publicity jaunts for *Neighbours* and I remember a press officer at an event at the InterContinental Hotel in Sydney offering me a line. Being a bit of a pothead I wasn't shocked, for once you have crossed that line with drugs and stopped seeing them as a great taboo then you have already climbed your first hurdle and are pretty much up for anything. So I took

David and me singing a Japanese version of 'Sealed with a Kiss' in the jungle. I really had a soft spot for that man. I think he was and has been misjudged. Amazing how perceptions are one thing and reality another.

I'm a Celebrity... changed my career. Here I am as 'Jungle Jase' plucking a yabbie from the camp stream. We decided not to eat it but it was one of the happiest days I spent in the jungle.

Dad, Zac, Jemma and me straight after the final of *I'm a Celebrity*. Dad had flown up from Melbourne to watch the last few days and spend some time with the kids.

It was pure heaven, having just spent three weeks in the jungle with a bunch of celebs, to be reunited with my family.

My recent tour, 2007. I put a lot of time and energy into this and was very proud of the final result, as it captured the essence of my music.

Concert for Diana. Singing at Wembley Stadium to a live crowd of 63,000 people and a television audience of 500 million viewers worldwide was insane. If this was it, career-wise, then I think I could die a happy man.

Concert for Diana. The energy backstage was incredible. What a wonderful way to celebrate a life – through the power of music and entertainment. One of the real highlights of my life.

The family was invited to No.11 Downing Street in September 2006 and I couldn't resist asking the policeman to take a photo of the kids in front of No.10 on our way past!

Ange took this of the kids and me on a walk in Woolstone. We rented the country pad so we could spend more time out of town. I relax when I'm not in London and the kids have space. This is me at my happiest.

Ange, the kids and me in Plymouth 2006.

Ange and me taking time out to relax at the country pad.

it. Well, hey, why not? You're only young once, I reckoned. From the moment I snorted the powder and tasted its slightly medicinal, antiseptic flavour as it coursed from my nasal passage down to the back of my throat, I realised that this was a drug for me. I liked the initial kick it gave me, that boost of confidence, the injection of energy. Within just a couple of minutes the drug took hold of me and got me into the party spirit, and even though I had just one line that evening it kept me going throughout the night. I didn't return to my room until sometime after six in the morning.

I knew there and then that this was a drug I could get a taste for, but cocaine was quite hard to come by in Australia during that era. It was on the scene in Sydney, but you didn't see much of it in Melbourne and it was regarded then as a rather exotic substance, something only the very rich, famous and outrageously decadent did. Taking cocaine was very New York, very Miami: it was for actors and actresses, rock stars and models, big city shakers and mafia types. It wasn't something you did back home in the suburbs in between turning the ribs and prawns on the barbeque. So my use of the drug back then was quite sporadic. If I came into contact with it and was offered a line I would accept, but I didn't go out of my way to find it and I certainly never bought my own supply. As it turned out that was probably a good thing, for by the time cocaine reached our shores it had travelled so far, been cut so much and was priced so highly that it was hardly worth taking. Frankly, you could get a bigger hit from a puff on a Ventolin inhaler than you could from an Australian gram.

It wasn't until I moved to London that I really became exposed to cocaine, for at the beginning of the Nineties the drug was everywhere and everyone seemed to be doing it. Taking coke in this city wasn't just socially acceptable, it was fashionable. These were the Brit Pop years, the days of Grunge, when musicians not only wrote and sung about getting out of it, they actually *were* out of it, and they didn't try to hide it either – if anything they broadcast it. This was the moment in time when the byword in fashion was Heroin Chic. If you wanted to be à la mode then you had to look like you were on drugs even if you weren't. Life in London was swinging at the time, and we were on the cusp of Cool Britannia. Nights at the Groucho Club, dancing at Subterranea in Ladbroke Grove, hanging out at home listening to house music or the Stone Roses or watching *The Word*, all of this was punctuated by lines of coke. If ecstasy was the drug of choice in the mid to late Eighties, at the turn of the decade it became cocaine.

I remember being quite taken aback as to just how commonplace cocaine use was when I first moved to London. Back at home coke was really only available on a certain circuit and it was something that was very much done behind closed doors, but over here everyone I came into contact with seemed to be doing it – and quite openly. You'd go round to a friend's house in the early evening and, much in the same way that you might be offered a beer or a glass of wine, they'd ask you whether you wanted a line. You'd be at a dinner party and no sooner had you put down your knife and fork than the cocaine would suddenly appear at the table like it was a Wall's Vienetta or the Australian equivalent, a Gaytime ice cream. At clubs around town, people would be pairing up and heading off to the toilets together for their little fix of white powder. At recording studios, musicians and technicians alike would get stuck in, to keep them going through their sessions – although I hasten to add that this never happened at Stock, Aitken and Waterman, for they were vehemently anti-drugs. The raciest thing that ever happened there in between sessions was a game of ping-pong. But, all in all, it was quite an eye opener for me.

In the early Nineties I kept my cocaine use to a minimum. Unlike smoking dope, which was something I was happy to do on my own at home, I equated taking cocaine with going out, with partying and clubbing, but in my early days as a pop singer I didn't have much of a social life, for I was always either in the studio or on the road. Sure, I was a big pothead. I never liked to be without my stash and there were few things I enjoyed more than getting stoned. It drove Richard mad at times, especially when we were travelling abroad together.

'Please don't tell me you are carrying anything on you?' he'd say, as we made our way to the airport.

'Of course not!'

'Well, you better make damn sure, Dono. You know how scatty you are. Just do me a favour and check your pockets, diary and wallet, and your wash bag, and make sure you're clean, mate. I really don't want the headache or embarrassment of you being hauled up by Customs. I can see the headlines now ...'

As into dope as I was, even I had my boundaries. Work always came before play. If I had a particularly taxing week ahead of me then I'd lay off the pot and my dope-box would be stashed away to the back of the drawer until my schedule was free enough for it to come out again. I didn't want to have a foggy head in the mornings, especially if I had an interview to do. I knew I couldn't have puffy eyes if I was going on a photo shoot, and turning up to a live kids' TV show being even faintly out of it was an absolute no-no. As I used to joke to Richard, the BBC's Saturday morning show was called *Going Live* not *Going Wired*. So I always kept a lid on it.

In my first couple of months on *Joseph* I stayed well away from drugs, and it wasn't until I found my feet on the show and felt that I knew the part back to front that I started smoking again. Even then I was restrained in my use. Just a couple of puffs at the end of the evening to counterbalance the adrenalin that still charged round my body after a performance. The way I saw it, having a spliff at night after a show was no different to having a glass of wine or two – in fact, aside from the effect it had on my vocal cords, one could argue that it was a darn sight healthier. By most people's standards I was living a monk's life, for there were a lot of boozers in theatreland in those days, and they weren't just for knocking it back after work either. For a lot of actors, having a quick glug on the old bottle of single malt to 'steady one's nerves' was the only way they could make it up on stage.

However, after all the furore of *The Face* debacle I started to use cannabis more heavily. As soon as I got in at night from the theatre the first thing I did was to roll myself a joint and settle down on the sofa, and I would smoke the whole thing down to the filter in one go. It was the only way I could cope with what was going on in my life at the time. It numbed the pain, calmed my nerves and was the one thing that could get me to sleep at night during that period. All I wanted around this time was to get completely out of it, for I simply couldn't deal with reality any more. And it was then that I really got into coke.

What I liked about cocaine back then was the sense of bravado it gave me. After a couple of lines any feelings of self-doubt or anxiety were quickly erased. On coke I was king of the hill, master of my own destiny, ruler of the universe, and, frankly, the most interesting person in the room. I could talk about myself for hours on end. 'Anyway, that's enough about me, let's talk about you and what you think of me ...'

I remember the first time I took it, around April 1992, for with the encouragement of my friends I'd decided that it was time to show my face in town again, if you'll excuse the pun, and after the Saturday-night curtain call I'd hooked up with a gang of them at one of my favourite haunts, a club called Billion Dollar Babes on the Tottenham Court Road, which was hosted by Graham Ball and Davina McCall. Billion Dollar Babes was *the* venue to be seen at that summer. It was cool, it was decadent, it was achingly hip. There were chill-out rooms, a catwalk, people dressed as robots and large dollar signs everywhere. Bjork, Kate Moss and Nicole Kidman went, Brad Pitt hung out there; anyone who was anyone on the London scene queued for a place in the club that year.

I'd been a little apprehensive about going at first, fearful that someone might have a go at me, but there was a pretty friendly bunch of people in the house that first night. And yet I just couldn't get into the party spirit. I was exhausted from the show and still feeling quite vulnerable. Sensing I was out of sorts, one of our party asked me if I would like a little 'pick-me-up'. I stalled for a moment, wondering whether this was really the best thing to do, but in the end I decided to take him up on the offer. If I was going to get through the night I would need something to get me going, and I could hardly spark up a doobie in a public place.

I went to a cubicle of the men's toilets, locked the door, cut myself a line on the top of the cistern, and with a rolled-up note I bent over and snorted it. That initial hit gave me such a buzz, such a lift, that I immediately wanted another hit. It was exactly what I needed, what the doctor ordered, or would have done had he been a little more with it.

Throughout the night I continued to take the drug, and when the lights came up on the club I was on such a high that I didn't want the evening to come to an end. The next thing I knew I had invited everyone back to my place to continue the party, and we stayed up until the early hours of the morning listening to music, taking cocaine, setting the world to rights, and talking absolute crap but feeling that we meant it at the time.

'God, I love you, you're just so great!'

'No, you're the one who's great!'

'I love your work! Your new stuff, your old stuff ...'

'I think everything you do is just brilliant.'

'Really? Tell me more ...'

I hadn't felt this good, this happy, this full of energy and life for months. I liked this drug, it worked for me, it made me feel good about myself and my life. Sure, I knew that it was a Class A drug, I knew that it was illegal and that it could be addictive, but none of that mattered to me at the time. What counted was the way I felt when I was on it. So long as I kept my use of it under control, what harm could it possibly do me? I'd just use it from time to time, when I needed it. I wouldn't take it during the week when I was working, I'd simply indulge in the odd line or two on a Saturday night when the mood took me.

The funny thing about drugs is that when you first begin taking them you never for one moment think that you are going to end up addicted. You know all the perils, you've heard all the lectures, you've seen all those images of those hapless, spotty heroin addicts, but as you take that first puff of spliff, tab of ecstasy or acid, or line of cocaine, you never think for one moment that it could happen to you. Why would you? When you take your first sip of beer as a teenager, you don't assume that you will one day wind up as an alcoholic. When you start smoking you don't imagine you will ever get cancer, you just learn to turn a blind eye to the boldly printed warnings on the front of the packets.

And so, when you start taking drugs you think it's only a bit of fun, something to do at the weekend. You're convinced you've got your drug-taking under control. You tell your friends that it's just something you do now and then, when you're in the mood. It's just a bit of a laugh, you keep reminding yourself, and the more you do it the more you convince yourself that this is the case.

When I first started using and buying my own cocaine that year I didn't think that I had a problem, or would ever have a problem for that matter. Coke was something I did at weekends, and in that I was no different from countless other people who moved in the same circles as I did. We worked hard, we played hard, for that was our release. *Rack it up, Jason. Chop one out for me. Got any skins?* But none of us ever considered ourselves to be addicts. Sure, we liked to cane it from time to time, we liked to live it up, let our hair down and party, but it wasn't the be all and end all of our lives. So we burnt the candle at both ends at the weekend, but come Monday morning I was getting ready to head off to the Palladium and they were all at their desks, in their studios, on set or behind it, getting on with their lives.

But addiction is a strange beast, a disease that slowly creeps up on you without you even realising it is happening. I thought I had my cocaine use under control by confining it to the odd Saturday night when I was off work for forty-eight hours. I'd go out with my friends, take a couple of lines to boost me up and make me feel better, then we'd hit the clubs, and when they drew to a close we'd head back to my place. A couple more lines, a spliff or two to bring us down, and then I'd take myself off to bed to see if I could sleep. Most of the time, I couldn't. It was all a bit of harmless fun, I kept telling myself, nothing to worry about. I was in my early twenties, I could afford it. I was having the time of my life, enjoying my youth. But those Saturday sessions were fast becoming a regular occurrence, so much so that it reached the point where they had become the highlight of my week. I couldn't wait until the moment that I came off stage and got out of that loincloth, coat and wig. Now that I had my own supply I'd head to the toilet, cut myself one hell of a line and snort it all up in one go, always mindful to flush the toilet as I did so to prevent anyone from hearing me. And with that I would leave the theatre and head into the night, for all I wanted was to be out on the town – and out of my head.

Chapter Seventeen

Rak and Roll

'OKAY, JASON,' HE said to me as handed me the drugs. 'I'm going to give you what you want, but I want to be straight up with you because I consider myself to be a friend of yours, not just your dealer. By taking these three grams of coke you are now an addict, and I want you to be aware of that. This is a disease that will stay with you for the rest of your life, even if you get clean. It's like a bad mistress who just won't go away. She comes knocking at the door, waiting for you to answer.'

I remember that conversation well. How could I forget it? This wasn't my father calling me a drug addict, it wasn't Richard trying to pull me back into line – this was my dealer for goodness' sake. How bad had I become? Surely he had people on his books that were just as bad as me, if not worse. So I'd started buying my own drugs, two or three grams at a time, but I could afford to do that, and it was always better to have a few to hand than to find yourself caught short in the middle of a session. There was nothing worse than trying to locate a dealer who could come to you at two in the morning, for it always dampened the high.

We were in the living room of Chepstow Villas, and on the French antique table was a wad of crisp twenty-pound notes that I had taken from the cash machine that morning in order to make this transaction. For a moment I hesitated in going through with the deal, but in the end I found myself pushing the money towards him. It was Saturday night after all.

I have often wondered what constitutes an addict. Does a daily glass or two of wine in the evening to help you unwind make you an alcoholic? If you smoke a couple of joints a week are you a junkie? If you crave chocolate and find yourself eating a bar every day, do you have an eating disorder? I'm sure that there are some people out there who would say that these are addiction issues, or at the very least indicate a dependency, but in relation to my own intake of cocaine I really didn't believe I had a problem. I didn't think I was either addicted to or dependent on cocaine, because when it came to drugs I knew that I was able to take them or leave them. In my mind I was what drug counsellors call a recreational user, someone who takes drugs when they want to from time to time, when the mood suits them. Sure, I was a bit of a binger. I enjoyed my Saturday nights out, it was what I worked towards all week, but it was just one night out of seven. If I really had a problem with cocaine, if

I was an addict, I wouldn't be able to restrict myself in this way. The way I saw it, so long as my drug use didn't interfere with my work then I didn't have a problem, for it meant that I was in control. Okay, so maybe I was pushing the engine to its limits, but I was still driving the car, as I liked to put it.

While I was in *Joseph*, Saturday night was the one day a week when I was able to let off steam, to be myself and have some fun, and I was always determined to make the most of it. I was so well-versed in the show that I could have done it in my sleep, but that didn't mean that it wasn't hard work. It was physically taxing and not something you could do on a hangover after a heavy night out. And when you work on a show like that, giving it your all, day in, day out, you reach a point by the end of the week where you are so emotionally and physically drained that you feel almost devoid of your personality. Taking drugs, getting high, gave me my identity back. When I was on them I could put Joseph to bed once and for all, and start being Jason again. So Saturday nights became sacred to me, and I wasn't going to let anyone or anything stand in the way of me having a good time – especially not my dealer. I was entitled to some fun. God knows, I deserved it.

When I'd first signed up for *Joseph* I had only committed myself to a year on the show, but as it was going so well towards the end of 1991 Andrew had been keen for me to extend my contract. Long before I got into partying I'd been in two minds about it, and I wasn't really sure I could face committing myself to another year, for as much as I loved the part and enjoyed my work I was starting to get itchy feet.

I knew that Richard was keen for me to stay on. We'd made a lot of money from the show, and with the profits from its subsequent records and album it was clear that *Joseph* was a licence to print money. But he was also well-aware of my mood back then.

'There's no need to make your mind up now,' he told me towards the end of 1991. 'You're due some time off, so go off, have a break and mull it over.'

And so, with Richard and Andrew's blessing, in January that year I packed my bags and headed off to Sri Lanka to meet up with James, who was in between jobs.

Looking back, I think that Richard and Andrew just assumed that all I needed was a break from the show, and that once I'd recharged my batteries I'd be eager to get back onto that stage again. But I didn't feel like that at all. If anything the reverse happened. Being out in Sri Lanka, having some time off from the show, being able to chill out during the day and party every night, to wake up and go to bed when I wanted, to scooter out to the beach to have massages, all simply made me realise what I was missing out on. I wanted to feel free again. I needed to act and be my age. I wasn't going to complain about my career, I had been incredibly lucky – blessed even. But as I headed out into the surf with James and made our way into the warm waters of the Indian Ocean on our boards, I couldn't help but feel slightly trapped by my own success. I realised that I had needed this – the holiday, the sea, the wind in my hair, the sun on my back, and time with my best mate. I just wanted to be myself again.

I'd been feeling pretty confused about my life before I left for Sri Lanka. When I looked in the mirror as the make-up came off after each show I didn't really recognise myself. It was like looking at a stranger. Despite protestations to the contrary from my dresser, Tina, I was convinced that I could see faint lines appearing around my eyes, and the hair was definitely going. I'd find myself staring more intently at advertisements for trichology clinics in the newspapers and at tube stations, and that just depressed me further – for the man in the ad, with his new, full, thick head of hair, was always in his mid to late forties, whereas I hadn't even made it to twenty-five. I was getting older, which was mostly fine – the only problem I had with it was that I couldn't remember where my youth had gone.

So I decided to quit the show.

Although he was disappointed to be losing me, Andrew was pretty supportive when I told him of my decision on my return to London.

'Are you sure there is nothing we can do to tempt you to stay?'

I shook my head.

'Well, we will all miss you, you've been a great team player and that's a wonderful thing to be in theatre.'

I knew that I was going to miss them too, for as much as I thought it was time for my Canaan Days to draw to a close, I had been happy there.

I bowed out of *Joseph* at the end of May 1992, and after a couple of weeks off I got back to work. My first single with Polydor, 'Mission of Love', was due for release that summer, so there was a lot of promotional work to be done for that, and we needed to put the final touches on the album *All Around the World*. I was relieved to be out of the show. So much had happened during that time, and I realised I had overstretched myself. I didn't want to spread myself too thin, I wanted to focus solely on my music, make a success of that, and have some free time to myself.

Following a small tour of the UK and Europe, *All Around the World* was released in 1993. Although it was not the album that I had wanted it to be, it had come together in the end and was well received. But now that it had been put to bed, I suddenly found myself with nothing to do.

'What's next then?' I asked Richard

'I think it's time to get you into a film.'

'Has anything interesting come up?'

'Yes,' he said, rifling through a pile of papers on his desk. 'I've got a couple of things that might suit you, and the great thing about both of them is that they are Australian productions, so you could go back home for a couple of months.'

'What are they?'

'There's some low-budget film called *Rough Diamonds*, set in Brisbane, about a cattle-herder – a little ordinary if you ask me. And another called ...' Richard paused for a moment as he tried to locate the script.

'Ah, here it is ... *The Adventures of Priscilla, Queen of the Desert.*'

'That's an odd title for a film. What's it about?'

'It looks quite fun actually. It's about a group of trannies heading off on a road trip round Australia. Stephan Elliot, the director, is pitching it as "cocks on rocks",' he laughed. 'And they've approached some good people – Richard E. Grant, Michael Hutchence.'

'Richard, please tell me you are kidding!'

'No, why?'

'After everything that went on with *The Face*, you want me to go and star in a movie about transvestites!'

'Well, you never know, it could turn everything around. Your chance to prove you're not some kind of homophobe after all.'

'Jesus, Richard, the media would have an absolute field day over that one. I've spent the last few months of my life trying to put all that behind me, and now you want me up there on the big screen in stockings and suspenders. Do you really want me to commit career suicide? No, I'll go with the cattle flick.'

'But you haven't even looked at the scripts yet!'

'I don't have to, I already know that's the winner in the race. A good old-fashioned Australian story, can't go wrong with that formula. Trannies on a road trip, give me a break!'

Now, I've made a couple of bad calls in my time, but I have to say that was probably my worst. When *Priscilla, Queen of the Desert* first screened at the Cannes Film Festival in 1994 it caused a near riot, and the following year it went on to win a string of awards, including an Oscar, a couple of BAFTAs, gongs from the Australian Film Institute and plaudits for its three main leads – and it would be this film that would take Guy Pearce, my old friend from *Neighbours*, who stepped into my shoes when I turned the role down, to Hollywood. *Rough Diamonds*, released that very same year, bombed.

But, hey, I don't have many regrets in life, and the way I like to see it now is that if I hadn't worked on *Rough Diamonds* I would never have met the film's producer, who to this day is one of my closest friends. I liked Jonathan Shteinman from the moment I met him, and we had some great times on location up in Toogoolawah, west of Brisbane, that August. Though he was that much older than me, Jonathan was one of the boys. He liked to have a good time and was always up for some fun. We quickly discovered we had friends in common back in Melbourne and that we shared the same outlook and sense of humour. But there was a serious side to Jonathan as well. Having trained as a lawyer before moving into the film industry, he had a sharp mind and a good eye for business. He liked making money, he wasn't embarrassed about success, and this meant something to me, for aside from Richard there were very few people I could talk to about my career. I felt embarrassed discussing my affairs with my contemporaries, for there was such a huge disparity in our finances – when I was doing *Joseph* I was taking home in a single week what most of them earned in a year. But with

Jonathan it was different: he liked talking about business, he was passionate about film, and I felt comfortable talking to him about work. He was to become something of a mentor to me.

Being of good Jewish stock, Jonathan was both impressed and amused that I was quite so careful when it came to money. I guess he thought that a boy my age would be happily running through it at a rate of knots, but when I earnestly explained that I really didn't want much from life and hoped to see my capital grow, he just laughed. 'Now I know that only I can make these jokes, but there'll always be a seat for you in the synagogue,' he joked.

It felt good to be out of London that summer and to be back home in Australia. In many respects, even though I was working it felt like a holiday. I enjoyed hanging out with Jonathan and the other guys on the set and we had a real laugh together, but when filming wrapped at the end of September I had to return to London, because I still had another single to release.

There was another reason as to why my trip to Australia that summer was good for me, and that was because I had managed to lay off the coke for a couple of months. That wasn't out of any great intention on my part – had it been there for the taking and any good I would have happily indulged on a night off – but there was little point in even hunting it down, for if the coke was bad in Sydney, it was even worse by the time it reached Brisbane. It was cut so heavily you would have been better off trying to get your kicks from a couple of lines of Johnson's baby powder or crushed-up paracetamol.

I was sad to leave Australia, for I'd had such a good time there over those couple of months, but if I am going to be honest about it there was part of me that was looking forward to going back to London – for as shameful and as pathetic as this is to admit, I couldn't wait to get stuck into a really big session. As I fastened my seat belt on the aeroplane I started to make plans. I'd get into London, make a couple of calls to my friends and get them over, then I'd contact one of the long list of dealers I had in my address book and order some coke in. Maybe I'd buy a bag of grass too, just to be on the safe side, and with that thought at the front of my mind I reached into my pocket, took out a sleeping pill and swallowed it. I'd need all the rest I could get if I was to be partying in twenty-four hours' time.

Back in London I quickly returned to my old ways. On Saturday night I'd be out on the town again, and then it would be back to my place to carry on. Now that I didn't have to conserve my energies for the stage I could be more relaxed about everything. I didn't have to keep a watchful eye on the clock and have a throw-out time, for I was free to party all night if I wanted to, and I soon found my Saturday nights bleeding into my Sundays. I wasn't going to bed at two or three in the morning, I was going to bed at two or three the following afternoon, and sometimes I wouldn't go to bed at all. What was the point? I didn't need to be on form the following week. If I was a little jaded on a Monday that was okay, for I didn't have anything to do really. Sure, I had an album to work on, and there were various commitments I had to honour in regard to Polydor, but that was about it really. I could do as much partying as I wanted, and that felt bloody great. I didn't have to wait until Saturday either – I could go out and get out of it any night of the week, if and when the mood suited me.

The problem with all this was that I no longer had any boundaries. Other than the odd gig or studio session there was no structure to my day, no real work commitments to keep me from using. Work had always come before play in my mind, but I didn't really have anything to do during this time. I could turn to drugs whenever I wanted, and that's what I was increasingly starting to do. I didn't wait for Saturday night to come round, I didn't have to have a reason to use – I didn't even have to have my friends around me, for I'd discovered that I quite liked taking coke on my own.

Alone, I felt I could explore my creative side. During these one-man sessions I'd put on my music, turn it to full volume and lay out my art materials and paper on the table, then I would start drawing away. Pen-and-ink sketches washed over with watercolour, powders, make-up, anything I could put my hands on – snot from my nose, blood from the pinprick I had made in my finger. I liked to write too. I'd pen reams of songs, all of which I thought were exceptionally brilliant at the time, but which were of course nothing more than tuneless and meaningless crap. I'd fill diaries with my thoughts and feelings. It was all quite abstract, dark and very sexual because that was how coke made me feel. As ugly as it may seem, on coke I liked to explore that aspect of my nature. When I reached a certain high I'd find myself poring over porn, thinking with my cock, as I would put it.

I enjoyed these periods of introspection, of finding myself. It gave me a sense of release. And I would carry on like this for hours at a time, until finally I'd exhausted both my creative juices and my stash of cocaine, and then I'd have to take myself off to bed with a couple of Rohypnol, for I was far too charged up to fall asleep of my own accord.

Few people, perhaps with the exception of my dealer, knew quite how bad my habit was back then. Richard knew I liked to get wasted but even he didn't see how out of control I was getting. How could he? He may have been privy to most aspects of my life, but he didn't know what I got up to behind closed doors in the privacy of my own home. I successfully managed to keep that part of my life away from people at that time. As far as they were aware I was just stoning it, they didn't realise I was using cocaine.

Keeping different parts of my life separate wasn't that hard, for I didn't look like a drug addict. I have always maintained that you can get away with anything when you have a tan, and my trips to Sri Lanka, Australia and a break in Bali had seen to that. Even when I was bingeing I kept up with my exercise routine. Three sessions at the gym each week, a good long run when the mood took me, a swim at my local health club, for that always made me feel alive again. I've always believed that my sanity was kept in reasonable shape as a result of the positive feelings I got after a good workout. In those days I pushed my body to the extreme, and I was in pretty good shape all things considered. I didn't display any of the physical attributes that one normally associates with someone who does too many drugs. I didn't have dark shadows under my eyes, a bad complexion, unwashed hair, and I wasn't underweight. There was nothing of the Pete Doherty or Keith Richards about me. As far as anyone was concerned I was the golden boy next door, and even when I had the best part of a gram up my nose I still looked like butter wouldn't melt in my mouth.

I was having the time of my life towards the end of that year and was enjoying every second of my newfound freedom. Richard, however, was not having such a ball. There was still a lot of interest in me at the time, especially in my capacity as an actor, but he was having trouble getting me to commit to anything.

'Look, Dono, I'm not being harsh on you here because I know you needed a break and to let off a little steam after *Joseph* and everything, but do you think it's about time you got a bit of focus? I don't want to push you into anything but I think we've got to make some decisions about the year ahead. I've got various offers and I need to start getting back to people on them. So come on, tell me, what are your plans?'

I knew what my plans were, but I also realised they weren't going to sit too well with Richard. What I wanted was some time out. I wanted to recapture my youth and live life to the full, and if that meant getting off the treadmill of stardom for a while then so be it.

At that point in my life I was determined to make up for the lost years and do all the things I felt I had missed out on during my teens. I wanted to travel and see the world, I wanted to hang out with people my own age, stay up late at night, sleep in all day, spend my weekends lazing around and my evenings setting the world to rights. I wanted time to be able to read, to think, to formulate my ideas and opinions, to get a little political or radical even. In short, I wanted my life back. I'd spent so much time in the limelight, projecting a certain image to the world, that I hadn't had time to grow up, and by my mid-twenties I wasn't really sure who I was. I was struggling with my identity and needed to go out there and find myself, even if it meant experiencing something of a delayed adolescence.

'I can see where you are coming from, Dono, but I am not sure this is the right time for you to take a break. It could do your career a lot of harm,' Richard warned me, but I chose to ignore him. I was tired of working, bored of being in the spotlight, I just wanted some time out. I had more than enough money in the bank to see me through, and when I had tired of leisurely life I'd get back to work, for with the arrogance of youth I just assumed that I would always be in demand, that people would want me. There would be another record deal on the table, another script with my name on it, another *Joseph*, for that's the way it had always been, and with that I closed the door on my flat in Chepstow Villas and my London life, and headed back to Australia for the New Year.

Chapter Eighteen

Crashing the Car

THE FIRST TIME I collapsed in public was at the Redhead nightclub in Albert Park, Melbourne, in March 1994. The following day, when the press and public asked what had happened to me that night, I let it be known via the grapevine that I had suffered from an asthma attack. When I slumped onto the dance floor at Billion Dollar Babes in London just four months later, I claimed that I had merely fainted, asserting that it had been hot and stuffy in the club that evening. And as far as anyone else was concerned, the night I fell on top of Jack Nicholson at someone's apartment, nearly taking him to the ground with me, I'd just had a 'little too much champagne', even though I still didn't drink.

Following the incident at the Viper Rooms in January 1995, I left it to Richard to make my excuses. 'It's all over the top,' a spokesperson from the company told the *Sun* newspaper when they got wind of the story and rang my management to follow up on it. 'He'd flown in from Sydney to LA, gone straight to the party and had been up all night.' When the paper asked whether I had a drug problem, my spokesman Tony and my assistant carefully deflected the question. 'He's always swimming and running. You couldn't find a healthier specimen,' they said.

It always brings a wry smile to my face when I read about celebrities having to be admitted to clinics on the grounds that they are suffering from 'exhaustion'. From my own experience I know that when you are in the public eye you can hardly put your hand up and admit to having a serious drink or drug problem, not if you ever want to work in the industry again. It's not a case of it being frowned upon, for most music and movie executives know exactly what the score is – it's just that you become uninsurable, and as such unemployable, and so on the celebrity circuit there is a vocabulary of euphemisms on hand to explain away these rather delicate situations.

In my case we didn't use the word 'exhaustion'. I 'fainted', I had 'asthma', I was 'jetlagged', 'had too much sun' or 'too much champagne', and when rumours started to circulate suggesting I was an epileptic I did little to dispel the myth. Although I suffered from seizures I knew full well that they weren't brought on by epilepsy, for my medical history said as much. They were drug-induced, pure and simple, brought on by what had become my seemingly insatiable appetite for cocaine.

Not everyone who is addicted to coke suffers from seizures – in fact it is actually quite a rare side effect of the drug – but for some reason I fell into that small percentage of people who regularly fit when they are on it. I've never really got to the bottom of why that was, my only reasoning being that at the height of my abuse I just didn't know when to stop or where to draw the line. When I was using I just wanted more and more of the substance, there was no limit to my intake. I'd be on it for days at a time, neither sleeping nor eating over that time, for it is impossible to do either, and I would carry on like this until I finally pushed myself to the point of collapse.

But, as much as I hated the fall, the fit, the seizure, and as frightening as these experiences could be, I still wasn't prepared to lay down the drugs, for I loved my cocaine. The very idea of it got me going. If I'd ordered some in that night from a dealer I would count down the minutes until they arrived. If they were running late for some reason I would start to get anxious and would keep calling their mobiles trying to establish a fixed ETA, and it wasn't until I finally had that wrap of cocaine in the palm of my hand that I could start to relax. I'd set that little package down on the table before me and unfold the paper with great care, mindful not to spill anything, and once I'd opened it I would stare at its contents with an almost childlike sense of wonderment, as though I had just unwrapped my very first Christmas present. Those little rocks of white crystallised powder, which in the right light seemed to glisten like uncut diamonds; that faintly chemical smell, which veered somewhere between bleach and petroleum, depending on where you had got it from; the texture of the drug itself, coarser than flour but finer than caster sugar – just having it in my possession gave me a kick and even made me gag. I'd wet my finger, dab it in the mound and take my first taste as though I was a wine connoisseur sniffing the cork of what one hoped to be a very fine bottle. If it numbed the tip of my tongue it had passed the test, I knew it was going to be good and at once I was happy.

I approached my cocaine use like a true professional. When I was on a binge I would go to great lengths to make the experience both as pleasurable and effective as it could possibly be. So as to make the most of each hit of the drug I took in a session, I would always make sure that my nasal passages were clear. It was pointless trying to inhale coke if your nose was blocked either by your own mucus or the residual coke that had crystallised there. If you wanted to maximise the effect of the drug then you needed to make sure it hit the membrane of your nose, and so with this in mind I'd steam, I'd sponge, I'd stuff tissues up my nostrils to clean them out – and once I had performed this ritual I was ready to go.

I suffered my first fit at the beginning of 1994, not long after I had freed myself from what I regarded to be the shackles of my career. With nothing or no one to hold me back, I took my partying to another level, and in the first few months of that year I lived every day as though it was my last. I spent January and February in Sydney and partied those months away in Bondi. Jonathan had a great, if slightly messy, apartment in the Empire Building on Campbell's Parade, right on the waterfront. I'd spend the day hanging out on the beach while Jono worked, and then at night we'd head out to the bars and clubs. It was summer in Australia and everyone seemed up for a party, which suited me down to the ground. We did the whole Sydney scene, hanging out with actors, singers, models, promoters, ad men. There was something to do every night of the week: private dinners at people's houses, VIP club nights, spur-of-the-moment barbeques, Mardi Gras. From Sydney I headed to Melbourne to spend some time with my family and old friends, and from there I went to Bali to catch some sun and surf before heading back to London. Back on my old stomping ground I started to live an almost vampire-like existence. When night fell I'd find myself in the back of a black cab heading off to the capital's numerous nightspots in search of fun: Billion Dollar Babes, L'Equipe Anglais, Subterranea, the Globe, the Groucho, Trade. I was such a regular at Brown's at the time that I've often thought that when I die they should do me the honour of placing a blue plaque over the door saying, *'Jason Donovan: actor, singer and total nutcase, resided here 1994–98'*.

Few people close to me begrudged the fact that I was on this extended holiday. Knowing what pressure I had been under over the last two years, Marlene thought that I should take some time out and try to get in touch with myself. She encouraged me to treat it as though it was a sabbatical. 'Read books, travel the world, broaden your horizons, take control of your life, Jay,' she said to me. Even Dad was pleased that I was taking a break, although true to character his reasons were very different from those of Marlene's. 'Find yourself? Come on, give me a break!' he barked. To him all that was just mumbo-jumbo. He wanted me to step back from my career for other reasons. Not only was he worried that I was heading for a burn-out, that I had experienced too much too soon, but he was only too aware of what the pressure of stardom could do to people, for in his time he had seen quite a lot of his fellow thespians crack under the strain of it all, and he was concerned that could happen to me. He wanted me to take some time out and approach my career with a long-term view and make some serious work choices. He thought it was good for me to get back to my roots for a while, and so when I announced that I was thinking of buying a place in Sydney towards the end of that year, he was delighted, if slightly jealous. Growing up, we'd always talked about owning a house or flat in Sydney. Finally, that dream was beginning to come true.

I had no intention of turning my back on London for good, for as far as I was concerned it had now become my home, but at this point in my life nothing was keeping me there. Earlier that year my contract with Polydor had been terminated. Although my album had got some reasonable reviews, it had not been the commercial success they'd wanted it to be, and for some time they had been quite sceptical about my future in the business. They simply didn't know where and how to place me in the market. I kept telling them that I didn't want to be just a pop act any more, but they couldn't see where I could go from there, for I had neither the integrity nor the material to be the kind of artist I wanted to become.

When they voiced this to Richard he played a deft hand and pushed them into a corner whereby they had to buy me out of our original deal. I wasn't that bothered – I'd made it quite clear to everyone that I didn't want to work that year. I'd lost all momentum. All I wanted was to put that roof rack on the car, strap on my surfboard and go and hang with the beautiful people.

'You want me to tell them that? In those words?' Richard asked.

'Why not? It's the truth.'

The fact was I didn't really care about anything any more, and, hey, at the end of the day I'd walked away from that situation a couple of hundred thousand pounds better off. With me gone to ground there was also no reason for Richard to stay in London, and so that year he packed up his offices and his family and headed back to Melbourne.

It was Jonathan who suggested that I got a place in Sydney. An apartment in his building had come up for sale and, sensing that Bondi was on the cusp of a property boom, he thought I should go for it. I didn't hesitate for a second, as I always trusted Jonathan when it came to financial matters and, like my father, I always regarded property as a sound investment. But it wasn't just about the money. I felt happy in Bondi at that time and wanted to be part of that scene, and I also knew that I couldn't keep imposing on Jono, for every time I came to stay he had to put me up in his office. He was trying to run a film production company from there, not a hostel for washed-up, crashed-out, burnt-out stars.

The apartment he had found for me was by no means swish, but it had a lot of charm. At the front it looked out onto the sea, and at the back onto the roofs and gardens of Bondi. When I opened the door to it for the first time I knew this was the place for me. I could spend time here chilling out and watching the world go by as I strummed away at my guitar. I could sit in the front room, writing, sketching and thinking, drawing inspiration from the Pacific Ocean. I'd hang out with friends and meet new ones. We'd go for coffees and something to eat in the numerous cafes and bars that lined the Parade. We'd head up to the north end of the beach and jump from the rocks. In the evening, maybe we'd come back to the flat, I'd get some beers in for my mates, roll a spliff, flick the cricket on and we'd sit there and watch the sun go down on Australia.

There was a real buzz about Bondi at the time. James Packer had already put money into the area, buying a sumptuous property south of mine on the Parade and investing in numerous shop fronts. The filmmaker Mark Joffe lived nearby. Toni Collette, Elle Macpherson and Naomi Watts were all living or residing in the neighbourhood. And this was a real plus for me, for not only were these people I knew, but being slightly more up the list than me it meant that when I strolled down the Parade people weren't that interested. They might clock me, but they wouldn't hassle me, for there were much bigger barramundi to be barbied on Bondi that summer.

It would be fair to say that at a certain point in my career this might have bothered me. When you have spent most of your adult life being screamed at and worshipped by your fans, and treated as some kind of idol, you take the adulation in your stride, to the point where you almost have a pen at the ready when someone asks for your autograph, or a comb in your back pocket because you never know when you might be papped. But at that stage in my life I simply wasn't interested in the attention. If anything I craved anonymity. I was sick of being constantly followed around and having my every waking move chronicled by the press.

I was by no means what anyone would describe as an 'A Lister', but in the UK for some reason pictures of me still held some kind of currency. When I had gone to Sri Lanka with James in 1992 and we'd headed out to surf one morning there had been a pack of paparazzi on the beach.

'What are they doing here?' James had asked.

'Fuck, I don't know,' I said with a sigh.

'It beats me, Jay. I just can't understand why they'd be interested in snapping you on your board? I mean, I'd get it if you were Mark Occhilupo, but let's face it you're hardly the greatest bloody surfer in the world. What's tomorrow's headline going to be then? *"Jason Donovan – surf sensation?"* They're off their heads.'

229

He wasn't that far off, for when the *Sun* splashed the story the next day they ran the photos with the headline: '*Jay Sun and Surf*'.

At the end of the day there are only so many excuses that you can give for your behaviour, and I knew that I was fast running out of lives. There are only so many occasions that you can hit the floor in a club and still pass it off as a fainting fit or an asthma attack. And yet, even though I sensed the press were on to me, and I knew I was in danger of being exposed, I still kept using.

My drug habit was no longer a secret among my group of friends, and while many of them were no stranger to a big night out they did wonder whether I was taking it to an extreme. 'Don't you think you should take it a bit easier?' they would say to me as they watched me plough my way through gram after gram. 'How about we call it a night?' they'd suggest. 'Save some for tomorrow?' But I never wanted to call it a night, or save some for tomorrow. For me it was all about the moment, seizing both the day and then the night, if that's what I wanted to do.

Line after line, gram after gram, night after night, until it got to the point where I could physically take no more and my body would simply have to shut down, to switch itself off, so that I would stop. I always knew when I was about to fit because I had learned to read the warning signals: blurred vision, a pumping heart, spatial disorientation and that strange sense of euphoria, as though as I was being anaesthetised, which hit me just before my legs buckled and I went down to the ground. From that point onwards I was blissfully unaware of what was going on. I didn't see my body spasm or convulse, my arms shake, my head thwack from side to side. I wasn't aware of the person hovering over me trying to turn me onto my side and pull my tongue from my mouth so that I wouldn't choke on it. I didn't hear the frantic calls being made to ambulances. Had I witnessed any of this then maybe, just maybe, I would have stopped.

Though in themselves these fits were never life-threatening, there were times when friends who witnessed them did wonder whether they would eventually lead to my demise. There was an incident when I came off the back of a scooter in Bali on Jalan Legion, and the night on that same holiday when I fell to the floor with such force that I split my head open, which at the time had rendered Jono, for the first time in his life, completely lost for words. Who was to say what would happen when my friends weren't around to hold me down, to pull my tongue from my mouth, to call an ambulance? I know it worried them all.

'The thing is, Jason – and listen, mate, I do mean this with the greatest respect ...' Jono began after the Bali episode. 'We're all *really* worried about you.'

Here we go, I thought, it's lecture time, Jono style.

'You see, mate ...' There was a long pause. 'I've got to ask, is there anyone there for you? Is there someone on hand to look after you? What if you'd been on your own that night, what would have happened then? Because,

Jason, and I have to be honest with you, I live in constant fear of the call …'

'The call?'

'The call from the police, in the middle of the night – the call to say something has happened to you.'

God, Jonathan could be an old woman at times. He was such a worrier, always fussing and fretting about something before it had happened. But in all fairness to him he did have a point. Before I'd taken possession of my keys to my pad in Sydney I'd had to bunk down in his office for one night, and I'd been so out of it when I finally crashed that I'd forgotten to blow the candles out. Unfortunately they'd been sitting on top of a milk crate in the middle of the room, and when that caught alight and subsequently melted and bubbled up, small droplets of boiling red plastic had spat out round the room, splattering the freshly painted walls of his office. It looked like Jackson Pollock had been round to decorate. When Jono had come in the next morning I was still comatose and lying on his sofa butt-naked.

'Mate? Mate? Are you okay?' he'd asked, prodding me in the back. 'Are you alive?'

I'd opened one weary eye and watched Jonathan as he surveyed what was left of his office and my debris from the night before. There were tissues on the floor, porn magazines on every surface, and on his desk – on top of his scripts, his paperwork and his financial forecasts – stood a bong.

I think this could easily go down as one of those breaking moments in a friendship, and had someone done that to me

I would have cut all ties with them for good.

But, rather than flying off the handle, Jono, bless him, had just apologised for finding me in that state. 'I'll come back when you've had a chance to get some clothes on,' he said, not really knowing where to look. 'It smells awful in here – plastic, maybe? And by the way, mate, I can hear water running ... I don't suppose you left the tap running in the bathroom when you went to bed last night?'

It was obvious that my drug use was completely out of control at this point, but I simply refused to see it at the time. Taking drugs, getting wasted, became my answer for everything. I felt I couldn't function without them. It got to the stage where I believed I couldn't sleep without a joint before I went to bed, or that I couldn't have a good time unless I'd had a line. I simply wasn't able to deal with the reality of daily life unless I was out of it in some way. And it wasn't just weed and coke – with the exception of heroin I would happily experiment with anything that came my way, and the only reason I laid off heroin was because I didn't see the point in taking a drug that made you want to go to sleep, which in itself was hardly the best reason to stay away from smack. Despite what I thought at the time, the drugs were now in control.

Chapter Nineteen

I Can Hear the Grass Grow

'JASON DONOVAN, THE *former Neighbours star and one-time singing sensation, collapsed at a restaurant this afternoon on Bondi Beach ...*' announced the presenter on the National Nine News. '*The incident took place at around 1 p.m. this afternoon. Paramedics were called to the scene and shortly afterwards the twenty-seven-year-old star was taken to the Prince of Wales Hospital. Let's go live to the scene ...*'

'*He was waiting to be served, I think he wanted a pasta dish, or maybe it was a coffee, I can't remember,*' their on-site witness said.

'But it was Jason Donovan?'

'Of course! I'd know him anywhere, although he has changed a bit. Anyway, he's there waiting for his order and the next thing you know he's having a fit! He just fell back and starts fitting! He was shaking and everything, fell back, smashed into this glass cabinet, and the next thing I know there's an ambulance outside and he's being given oxygen, and then he's being driven off to the hospital …'

'Mate, come on, do you really have to watch this again?' asked Jonathan. He took the remote control from my hand and switched the television off.

'Why do they keep referring to me as "former" and "one-time"? The way they're carrying on you'd think I was dead.'

I was lying on my sofa in my flat on the Parade, feeling weak and bruised, not just from the fall but from the humiliation of it all.

'You're pretty close to it,' he laughed. 'Have you looked at yourself in the mirror lately?'

There was no escape from it now: everyone knew what was going on. This fall, this seizure, had been so public it had generated a lot of media interest. I hadn't collapsed in a nightclub, or at a private party or event, where a team of bouncers could usher me out of the back door to get me the help I needed. This seizure had happened in broad daylight, at lunchtime, when Gusto's, a popular cafe in Hall Street, was at its full capacity. There had been families in there – young kids, old women, like the one who'd just given her first-hand testimony to camera. As they sat drinking their coffees, eating their pasta and their salads, what must they have thought when this slightly dishevelled, pale and gaunt figure fell into the glass cabinet of soft drinks and started to fit?

Luckily for me, within minutes Jonathan was at the scene. By chance he'd stepped out of his office to get a take-away coffee, and the way he tells it he was slightly peeved to see an ambulance outside his favourite cafe, for there was a lot of commotion going on and he wondered whether he would ever get served. He was about to turn on his heel and find somewhere else to get his cappuccino, then stopped in his tracks when he saw me being lifted into the ambulance. Jonathan came with me to the hospital. As it was I didn't have to stay long. Once I'd been given the once-over by the doctors I was discharged and told to take it easy for the rest of the day.

So here I was on my sofa, once again feeling like a complete and utter bloody idiot. But unlike the other times when I had fitted I knew that this time I wasn't going to get away with it. I couldn't pass this one off as a fainting fit, or an asthma attack, or say I'd had too much sun. You only had to look at me to know I hadn't seen daylight for weeks. I may have had a tan from being on the beach but there was no escaping the fact that I looked tired. The whites of my eyes were bloodshot and there were dark circles under them. What was left of my hair was lank, my cheeks were hollow. I was no longer the bright-eyed blond-haired kid I had once been. In fact, I didn't feel human, it was like life had been drained from me. I looked and felt like some kind of *Thunderbirds* puppet.

Of course, I had no one to blame for this but myself. I must have been up 'partying' for two or three days – I couldn't remember. I'd felt okay as I walked into Gusto's to get my coffee – well, as normal as you can feel when you have a quarter of an ounce of cocaine coursing through your body – and I'd been standing patiently in the queue waiting to be served, but as I made my way to the counter I started to convulse. I tried to reach out to steady myself, but there was nothing to grab hold of and it all happened so quickly that I couldn't make it down to the floor. The next thing I know I'm awake, lying on my back with my head in the soft-drinks cabinet, covered in tiny shards of broken glass, and there is a medic crouched over me trying to put an oxygen mask on my face.

It was 1995. So far I had tried to keep my cocaine addiction secret, and to date I had somehow managed to get away with it, but now my time was up. Although no one was going so far as to stand up and call me a junkie, the inference was there. You only had to read between the lines. On television that night they referred to me as being 'troubled', and in the press the following day they catalogued the various seizures I'd had that year – although I noted that they missed quite a few – and talked about my increasingly erratic behaviour and my fading career. 'What happened to Jason Donovan?' the columnists asked. 'The golden boy of stage and the small screen ... the glittering career he once had ... *Neighbours* ... *Joseph* ... Kylie Minogue.' At that point I stopped reading.

The press and the general public may have only just got wind of my 'problem', as they called it, but my family had been aware of it for some time. When I had collapsed on the dance floor at Redhead's the previous year, Brian Goldsmith, who co-owned the club with his son and my close friend Brett, had called Dad to tell him what had happened. When I was discharged from the hospital I had returned to my house in Wellington Street and found my father waiting for me on the doorstep. The look on his face said it all. It was that sense of despair that only a parent could have for a child. I knew there was little point in attempting to pull the wool over his eyes, trying to pretend that I'd had an asthma attack, for Dad had suffered with the condition for forty years and he didn't go around keeling over or fitting in nightclubs. And, in any case, there was little point trying to make excuses, for Brian, who was an old mate of his, had put him in the picture. For some time Brett had been worried about my state of mind. As a club owner he was up for a party, for that was his business after all, but in all his years of being on that scene he hadn't come across anyone who took it as far as I did, and it had worried him. That night, as I'd slumped to the floor and started to convulse, it had been Brian and Brett who had driven me to hospital.

'I just don't understand why you would do this to your-self, Jason,' Dad had said. 'You've got so much going on in your life, so much to live for. Why would you want to throw it all away on this ... these drugs?'

I didn't reply. Well, what could I say?

'Do you need help? A doctor? Some counselling? Just tell me what you need and I'll sort it out for you.'

Marlene was equally as concerned. Unlike Dad she had seen me when I was high on drugs, and as liberal as she was, when I'd turned up at her house one morning after an all-night bender she had been shocked. Unable to stay with me as she had to leave for work, she'd told me to stay there while she was out for the day and get some rest. When she had returned from work that afternoon I had been lying in my underwear on the top of her bed, passed out. I'd known that Marlene always kept some sleeping pills on her, and while she was gone I'd been through all her drawers, rooting about like a burglar, throwing all her clothes around, until I eventually found them. I'd taken a fistful of them, as though they were M&Ms, and then conked out.

When I'd come round she had tried to talk to me there and then about my addiction, but I wasn't having any of it. I was dismissive with her and told her to mind her own business.

'Jesus, Jay, what's happening to you?'

'What do you mean by that?'

'You used to be such a warm-natured person, so kind and sweet, and now you're so on edge and aggressive all the time. It's all just so selfish and ugly. These drugs are eating into your personality. It's not good, Jay. It really isn't good. All you think about is yourself.'

Later that year we had gone on a holiday to Bali together. Although she hated flying, Marlene had been excited about the trip as she hadn't had a break in ages, so I had treated her to the vacation and had even booked us into Business Class.

'Don't be late for the airport,' were her last words to me when she telephoned the day before we were due to leave.

'You know how nervous I get travelling, I want you there to hold my hand.'

I agreed, because I knew only too well how much she hated flying. God love Marlene, but this woman does not travel well, to the point where she can't even do bridges. She's the type of person who will add an hour onto her journey and circumvent Greater Melbourne so as to avoid having to cross the Bolte Bridge.

But, despite knowing all this, I was, of course, late for the airport that morning. So late, in fact, that had we not been travelling Business Class and if Marlene hadn't pleaded with the airline officers, we wouldn't have made the flight at all. I had been up all night and had taken my last line of coke just before I got in the cab to take me to the airport. Even though we were heading to a tropical island I was dressed in an overcoat and had a beanie hat on my head. I was unshaven and smelled of stale tobacco from all the grass I'd smoked.

'Look at the state of you! Have you been to bed?'

'No ...'

She had been furious with me, and her mood hadn't improved by the time we took our seats in the cabin of the plane. I was wittering on, complaining that I was cold, shivering so badly she had to ask the flight attendant for more blankets. I was supposed to be looking after her on this trip, holding her hand as the plane took off, and there she was now having to take care of me.

'I just don't get it with you. You have this great life, this wonderful soul, a whole bunch of people who love and adore you, and you have to destroy it all. What is it with you ... this act of rebellion? Why are you so intent to walk on the dark side of life? What exactly are you trying to prove? I just don't know you any more, Jay, I really don't. You're acting bizarrely, you talk absolute rubbish ... you might think you are being cool, but no one else does. If anything you are becoming something of a joke!'

As harsh as her words were I knew that she was telling it as it was. She was trying to give me the wake-up call I needed, trying to push me into a corner, to make me see things for what they were. But the truth hurts, and as she carried on I couldn't stop myself from welling up and tears began to pour down my face. Marlene took my hand and gave it a squeeze.

'Jay, you do know I am only saying this because I love you.'

Mum had been equally as concerned about me and was keen for me to get professional help. But when she called to tell me that she had found the name of a good psychiatrist, I didn't want to know and simply changed the subject.

When you are addicted to drugs, that substance will always come before anything or anyone else in your life, and that's how it was with me. When Gran passed away from cancer in February of 1995 I was absolutely distraught. She had been everything to me – one of the greatest loves of my life – and I couldn't really imagine life without her. But not even my feelings for Gran could come between me and my addiction, for, as ashamed as I am to say this, on the day she was buried I'd been up all night and had used, and by the time I got to the funeral I was completely out of it, which is the single biggest regret of my entire life, something that I will never forgive myself for.

I was finding it increasingly difficult to maintain any kind of relationship at that point in my life. In 1995 I began seeing a girl called Erica Baxter. Erica was exceptionally beautiful, tall and lithe with these wonderful feline eyes. You couldn't help but be transfixed by her, and when we got together she was one of the leading models in Australia. At eighteen she was a good deal younger than me, but she was mature for her age. She came from a good family in Gunnedah. When we first started seeing each other I thought, 'This is it, she's the one, I don't want anyone else in my life', and in 1996 I persuaded her to come and live with me in London. I was crazy about Erica, but at the end of the day we couldn't make it work, for as much as I adored her, my love of cocaine always came first. Eventually she packed her bags and headed back to Sydney, much to her parents' relief.

Erica meant a lot to me, but we met at the wrong time, in the wrong place, and still to this day I feel guilty about what happened between us, because no one deserves an addict for a boyfriend. But I am not going to beat myself up about it, for I am a strong believer in fate, and she is now happily married to James Packer.

Despite my predilection for cocaine I managed to do some work over that period. In 1994 I starred in a television movie called *The Last Bullet*, which had been commissioned for Channel Nine in Australia. I had a part in another film called *The Sun, the Moon and the Stars* and acted in a couple of stage plays, *Camelot* and *Night Must Fall* (and my God it did). But, if I'm honest about it, none of it was great. I didn't exactly have Stephen Spielberg, David Geffen or Trevor Nunn on the other end of the phone begging me to come and work with them. Such was the radio silence when it came to work that sometimes it felt like I could hear the grass growing.

I realised that I was fast becoming recognised for one thing only, and that was drugs. I'd read articles about myself – of the 'Where are they now?' variety – and all they ever seemed to concentrate on was my seizures.

'Why is it, Jono, that Liam Gallagher can snort as much bloody coke as he wants and no one seems to give a damn, but I fall over in clubs a couple of times and it becomes news?'

'Mate, that's the whole point. You're not Liam Gallagher or Keith from The Prodigy, you're Jason Donovan. It just doesn't fit with your image, that's precisely why it is news.'

Tired of the constant speculation as to what was 'wrong' with me, I decided, in a fit of madness – and quite a lot of drugs – to go on the record. Everyone was talking about it as it was, so I might as well have my say, I reckoned. So when I was asked in a radio interview why I took drugs, my response was simple yet honest. 'Because I like them,' I said. The following day my admission was all over the front pages of the papers.

Now that it was out in the open I thought I would go for it. Why not? Why should there be one rule for Liam and another for me? In the months that followed I would tell anyone who listened that I had experimented with drugs. I made it clear that I didn't advocate or condone drugs; I simply let it be known that I had used them. My justification to the press, and indeed to myself at the time, was that I was an artist and as such needed to explore my personality and anyway, no one's perfect!

'Without drugs there would never have been *Great Expectations* or *Alice in Wonderland*,' I rather pompously declared in one interview, which was brave of me since I hadn't the faintest clue what I was talking about. Had Charles Dickens or Lewis Carroll used drugs, or was it Conan Doyle? Who cared, it sounded good!

I would argue, though not advocate, that drugs can sometimes influence creative artistic activity. 'You only have to look at Paul McCartney and the Beatles to realise that.' I was on better ground there, but that was hardly going to bring the interviewers round to my point of view, for it was blatantly clear to everyone that I certainly wasn't Paul McCartney, and neither was I Mick Jagger.

When a journalist challenged me on this, pointing out that I had never written any of my own material and suggesting that in my capacity as a one-time teen idol I owed it to the youth of today to set a good example, I was unrepentant.

'People make mistakes. Life isn't a perfect Andrew Lloyd Webber musical!'

'Oh, that's just marvellous, Dono, just bloody marvellous! How do you think Lloyd Webber will react when he sees that?' Richard said to me when he read the article.

'You know what, Richard, who cares? It's me. That's what I think.'

I thought that by admitting my drug use I would gain some kind of street cred that would change the way people saw me, but in fact the reverse happened. I didn't look cool at all, I just came across as really rather sad and slightly lost. I believed that I could turn the game around, but it was beyond my control.

Now that my drug use was out in the open, my family became more determined than ever to get me to seek professional help, but I refused to see reason. I didn't want to go to counselling, to see a shrink or a therapist. Why would I? They would only tell me to stop taking drugs, and that was not what I wanted to hear at that point in my life. I think that by that stage Richard had pretty much given up on me, and as far as Jonathan and James were concerned they were aware that they were treading on thin ice. If they pushed me too far, started telling me things I didn't want to hear, they knew that I would cut them out of my life for good, and they realised that in the long run this could be more dangerous for me. At least while they kept their own counsel they were still in my life and could keep an eye on me. If anyone so much as broached the subject of my drug addiction with me I would fly off the handle, stop taking their calls and would effectively freeze them out, as I had done with both my parents by that point. Then I would take another line, for that was the only way I could cope.

The only person who stood up to me at this point was Brett. 'Get yourself together, Jason,' he said to me one afternoon in his studio in Commercial Road in Melbourne. 'If you don't care about what you are doing to yourself, then maybe you should start thinking about what this is doing to the people around you. Stop acting the pop star. I don't give a shit if you are rich or famous, mate, it means nothing to me, just pull yourself together!'

His words stung, to the extent that I decided to shut the door on life in Melbourne once and for all, and sell up.

Unsure of what to do next, of how to get through to me, in 1998 Dad wrote an open letter to me, which was published in *Woman's Day* magazine.

'Dear Son,' it began. *'It breaks my heart to look at pictures of how you are now. On more than one occasion I warned you that you were killing yourself, I even got the name of a detox specialist but you were in denial. You had the attitude, "Don't worry – I can handle it …"'*

I only got as far as the first paragraph. I didn't have to read on, for I'd heard it all before.

Chapter Twenty

Ange

FROM THE VERY first moment I laid eyes on her I was intrigued. It's not every day that you come across a girl working in stage management, for the back line of theatre has for some reason always been a predominantly male profession. And as I watched her go about her work, taking control of the production team, refusing to take any nonsense from anyone, I was at once struck by her self-assurance, her poise and her strength of character.

I met Angela Malloch, or Ange, as she prefers to be known, when I was starring in the lead role of Frank N. Furter in the UK tour of *The Rocky Horror Picture Show*. So it wasn't *Joseph*, the production wasn't headlining at the Palladium in London, and I knew full well when I signed up for the fourteen-month tour that neither Shirley Bassey, Elton John nor Liza Minnelli were going to be in the front row when the show opened in Birmingham in 1998, but it was a good production and, frankly, I was both happy and lucky to be working again. However, as I squeezed into my basque every night and put on my stockings and suspenders, I couldn't help but see the faint irony in it all, for had I been brave enough to take on the role of a transvestite in *Priscilla, Queen of the Desert*, who could say where I would be now – sipping Long Island Iced Teas by a pool in Hollywood perhaps? But the hand of fate is a strange thing. So maybe I'd missed out on the big movie career, but I could live with that, for had I taken that role I would never have met Ange.

My feelings for Ange rather took me by surprise, for on the face of it she was so unlike any girl I had been attracted to in the past. She never wore make-up, she didn't bother with her hair, and she lived in a simple uniform of jeans and T-shirts – in fact, when we first met she didn't even own a skirt. If I were to be completely honest, she was a bit of a tomboy. She liked her beer – in a pint glass of course, for there were no half-measures for her – and she loved her sport. She was an avid football fan, supported Newcastle United, and in her teens she had played for Oxford United's women's team – she even had the trophies to show for it.

As far as Ange was concerned, she was who she was, and she made no excuses for it. She wasn't going to doll herself up for anyone. What you saw was what you got with Ange, and if you didn't like it then tough, you could sling your hook. But Ange didn't need powders and paints to make her attractive, or a wardrobe full of designer clothes for her to stand out from the crowd, for she had the most beautiful face and figure. In her jeans and T-shirts, with her hair scraped back from her unpainted face, she was so natural. She was absolutely gorgeous. It's hard to explain, but she had something about her, something that drew me in. She had an inner beauty.

As much as I was physically attracted to Ange, what really drew me to her was her personality. I have always been a great admirer of strong women. Both Gran and Marlene shared that attribute, which is why I was always so close to them both, but I'd never in my life encountered anyone quite so steely as Ange. This girl was not to be moved by anyone, or anything for that matter. She was exceptionally determined in everything she did. Nothing fazed her, nothing seemed to bother her, and if it did she never let it show.

Ange had come from quite a modest background. Born and raised in Oxford, she had grown up on a council estate and been educated at the state comprehensive, and she had worked hard at school to get to where she was now. She was naturally bright and always loved to read, and from an early age she had wanted a career in the theatre. To her credit, she achieved her goals. With just a couple of years of hard graft on the back line, here she was pretty much at the helm, deputy stage manager of a major touring production. The fact that she was working in a man's world didn't bother her in the slightest, for she could stand her own ground and give as good as she got. This girl took no prisoners. When we moved round the country she was perfectly happy to sleep in the back of the stage truck so that she would be ready for the 'load in' of equipment in the morning. 'It saves time,' she said to me one day. 'And in any case, it's pretty comfortable in there.' That was the kind of girl she was. For so long on the circuit I'd only come into contact with a certain kind of woman – you know: big hair, big bust, big attitude – but Ange wasn't like that, and she was a breath of fresh air. She was exactly what I needed in my life.

It took me a while to get to know her. She wasn't the type of person to be impressed by celebrity for she had worked in the business for too long. So I had a name, so what? The way she saw it I was just a cog in the machine of the production. The fact that I was in the show might help put some bums on seats, but at the end of the day that didn't help her in her job. She'd had to deal with a lot of grand egos in the past, and as far as she was concerned most actors could be more trouble and bullshit than they were worth. So when we were first introduced she didn't exactly stand on ceremony.

Working on any production, be it a play, a film or even a music video, is always a very intense experience, but it is nothing compared to being on the road. While I was in *Joseph* I had the benefit of going home to my own flat after each production and sleeping in my own bed, and I could see my friends and have time for myself, but with *The Rocky Horror Picture Show* I didn't have these luxuries.

You couldn't walk away from the production each night, slam your dressing-room door and go back to your own life, for this was your life, so you had to learn to make the best of it.

Throughout my career I had always made a point of getting to know my fellow cast and crew, of being 'one of the boys'. It was all well and good acting like the star of the show when you were on stage, but if you took that attitude with you after you took your final curtain call then you were in for a very lonely tour. So on *The Rocky Horror Picture Show* I went out of my way to be part of the team. I'd go to the bar with them after the show, I would spend time with them during the day. If someone organised a night in a club, a cast and crew football match or a dinner in a restaurant, I made a point of always being there even if I couldn't really face it.

There were moments when I was happy to be on my own. I'd switch on *Newsnight*, roll myself a joint and ring down for food – a cheese platter with pickles, for that was what Dad always used to order when he came back from a show when I was a kid. Here I was doing exactly the same as my dad. It was just like the Robbie Williams song 'Strong' where he talks about dressing like his dad and dancing like him when he's drunk. But I didn't want to do that every night. I needed to be with people. And yet, in this case, as much as I wanted to share in the camaraderie of the production and be a team player, I admit that I had ulterior motives, for I knew that this was the only way I was ever going to get to know Ange.

It didn't take long for us to hit it off. Once she realised that I wasn't some queenie luvvie and that I had no airs and graces she started to warm to me. We had a good time together and formed a friendship. But, of course, that wasn't enough for me. I didn't just want to be Ange's mate, another of her production pals, someone to have a quick drink with in the hotel bar after work. I wanted more than that, but my problem was I didn't know how to go about it. When I'd set my sights on someone in the past it never took me long to go in for the kill, but with Ange I stalled. I'm not sure why it was, but for some reason I just wasn't brave enough to make my move. I tried to send out signals to her but she was pretty unreceptive. I tried dropping hints, even flirted a little with her, but I think she just thought I was being friendly. When she celebrated her birthday with a party in a restaurant in Bradford I spent hours in a shop stewing over what to get her. In the end I settled for a Mambo T-shirt – well, I was hardly going to get her a dress – and when I gave it to her she simply smiled and blushed. 'Thanks, Jase. That's really sweet of you.'

She seemed so shy. How was I ever going to get through to this girl?

'You've just got to make your move,' Mark White, who played Eddie and Doctor Scott in the show, said to me one day. 'Be brave about it.'

'What if she knocks me back?'

'She won't.'

'How do you know?'

'Because she likes you.'

'Has she told you that?'

'Not in so many words ... this is Ange we are talking about here. She doesn't do heart-to-hearts! But I can tell she likes you. It's obvious. Go for it, mate.'

I know what I saw in Ange, but I haven't got a clue what attracted her to me. I was hardly in the best shape at the time, but I must have had something going for me, for when I eventually found enough courage within me to make my move and tell her how I felt, to my surprise those feelings were reciprocated and we began our affair.

It felt good being together. In many ways we offered each other a safety net, a comfort zone, during that tour. Ange gave me a sense of security and support, and took away the loneliness of the tour. She filled my days with happiness, my nights with warmth and love, and I was grateful for that, for it was a long tour. I was always trying to get her to stay with me at my hotel. As the 'star' of the show, I had the option of staying at a pretty good hotel in the area while the rest of the cast and crew didn't have such luxuries and had to find their own digs downtown. As much as she wanted to be with me I know this made her feel a little uncomfortable, but I was determined not to be apart from her so I was constantly trying to lure her back with me.

Ange knew from the beginning of our relationship that I took cocaine. While I didn't use the drug during the week when I was working, come the weekend I went for it hammer and tongs, just as I had done when I was in *Joseph*. Ange was a woman of the world and wasn't shocked by my drug use. In the circles she moved in, taking cocaine was common practice, and the way she saw it my Saturday-night binges were nothing more than that. So I'd get a little more wasted than most people, take more lines than most, but it was the weekend and she knew that I both needed and liked to let off some steam. As I wasn't using the drug during the week she didn't think that I had a serious problem, I was simply doing what countless friends did: taking cocaine on a recreational basis. It wasn't until she came to stay with me in London that she realised quite how extreme my drug use really was, but by then it was too late, for we were deeply involved with one another. When you are in a relationship you don't walk away from someone because they drink or smoke too much, or because they take too many drugs. When you fall in love with someone, part of you always believes that with enough support and encouragement you can help them. All you want to do is rescue that person, to save them from themselves and the demons that haunt them.

Now the only problem with this was that I didn't want to be saved or rescued. I liked taking cocaine. I didn't want to stop taking it and still refused to see that I had a problem. As strong as my feelings for Ange were at the time, I wasn't going to stop taking cocaine for her – or for anyone for that matter. I had everything under control. I could handle it, I told her. The fact that I didn't use during the week (well, not often anyway and certainly not while I was working) was proof in itself. That's what I kept telling myself.

Just as I believe that it is impossible to be genuinely in love with two people at the same time, when you are addicted to drugs trying to conduct a serious relationship with someone is completely unfeasible. For as much as you love the person you are with, however strongly you feel for them, your addiction to your drug will always come first. 'Like a mistress who comes knocking at the door and refuses to go away' is how my dealer had put it when he had warned me about my habit. I'd chosen to ignore what he was saying at the time, I couldn't really see what he was saying. But now I could. My mistress was cocaine, and I kept opening the door to her despite the fact that I was with Ange.

When the *Rocky Horror* tour came to an end, with nothing to do, with no structure to my day and no reason not to use, I slipped back into my old ways. When I'd split with Erica I had sold my flat in Chepstow Villas and moved to a mews house in Notting Hill, and there I'd sit holed up for days while ploughing my way through grams and grams of coke. As home for Ange was Oxford and we wanted to be together, she had come to stay with me, but as the months went by and I carried on like this, she simply couldn't cope.

'Something's got to give here, Jason,' she said to me one day. 'I can't live with you like this. You're destroying yourself, destroying what we have together. I can't have a relationship with you when you are like this.'

I heard what she was saying, but rather than see sense, rather than appreciate what I'd got with Ange, I am ashamed to say I chose the drugs over her. If something had to give then it was our love affair, for I wasn't prepared to drop the drugs, to leave my mistress, even for this beautiful, strong, clever woman who I'd pursued just months before. And so, cruelly, stupidly and selfishly, I told her to leave. She packed her things, walked out the door and went to stay with my assistant, Julie, who she had become close to.

I didn't have the mindset to think about what I had lost, to consider for a moment what I had done or to realise the hurt I had caused her. I was beyond emotion – the coke and my appetite for it had long put paid to that – and I used drugs to mask any pain I felt. If Ange wanted out, she wanted out. If she wanted to be with me she could, but she would have to take me as I was, and she wasn't prepared to do that, so good riddance. In many ways, being on my own suited me, as I'd become quite insular. I didn't want to have to think about other people, to have that burden round my neck. Even when my sister Katherine rang to say that she was coming over from Australia to visit and wanted to spend a couple of months with me, I viewed that as an inconvenience, even though I loved her with all my heart and hadn't seen her in over a year. All I wanted was to be on my own and to take my coke in peace. It was totally selfish of me, but I wasn't in control – the drugs were!

When Ange walked out of the door of the mews house, I thought she had walked out of my life for good, and with the way things had ended between us I really didn't expect to see or hear from her ever again. So when a letter in her handwriting appeared on my doormat one morning some months later, I was surprised. I left the letter unopened for an hour or two. I was feeling quite wrecked from the night before and the last thing I needed in my current state was to sit down and read the barrage of abuse that she had doubtless sent me. But when I did get round to reading it, later that morning, it wasn't what I expected at all. There was no recrimination, no angry words, no abuse, for Ange wasn't writing to tell me what she thought of me. She was writing to inform me that she was pregnant.

I must have read that letter twenty times that morning, over and over again, but I was still having trouble taking the news in. Ange said that she had taken the decision to keep the baby, and that while she didn't want or need anything from me, she thought it was only fair that I should know that I was going to be a father.

'A *father*.' One small word, but a lifetime of meaning. I'd never really thought about children before, that all seemed a lifetime away, even though I was now in my thirties. Of course, I wanted them, in the future, but not now, not at this juncture in my life. I mean, if I couldn't even handle having a relationship how on earth was I going to cope with having a child of my own. I wasn't ready for this, I didn't want this, it wasn't the right time for me. But I knew that I didn't have any choice in the matter. Ange had made it clear that she was having this baby no matter what, and I knew her well enough to realise that once she had come to a decision like this she wouldn't and couldn't be turned.

Knowing that Ange wouldn't take my calls, I rang Julie.

'She can't do this to me!'

'Well, she is, so you'd better get used to the idea, Jason. Whether you like it or not you are going to be a father. It's going to happen.'

I dealt with this piece of life-changing news in the only way I knew how – by getting completely off my head. I needed to get out of it, to escape from my reality, but when I eventually came down from my high I realised that I was going to have to confront the situation once and for all, and so I called Ange and agreed to meet with her.

She was pretty straightforward with me. She explained that she hadn't intended to get pregnant, but when she learned that she was and had this confirmed by her doctor she knew there and then that she was going to keep the child. Though she acknowledged that it wasn't the best of situations to find herself in, she was happy that she was pregnant and was looking forward to having the baby. She told me that she didn't expect anything from me, be it either financial or emotional support. She would raise the baby on her own, and if I didn't want to be part of its life she completely understood, but if I was to decide that I did want to be involved there would always be room for me.

I sat there in silence and listened as she spoke.

'I'm not asking for anything from you. I am just telling you how it is. You can walk away now and get on with the rest of your life and you never have to see me again, and if you do that I will respect you for it, but if you want to be part of our lives then you know where I am.'

I wasn't sure what to do. I was snookered. I was so confused by it all. I needed time out to clear my head and get my mind round this before I committed myself to anything.

'Take some time to think about it,' Ange said to me as she got up to leave. 'I'm not going to put any pressure on you either way.' And as she walked away I knew that she meant it.

Over the next few weeks I deliberated about what to do. I rang family and friends and asked them for their advice. I even consulted my doctor Peter Wheeler. 'You – a father!' my mother said when I rang to tell her the news. 'Jason, how are you going to bring up a child? You can't even look after yourself.' Dad was supportive, though like Mum he did question whether I was ready for it. He had met Ange while I was on *The Rocky Horror Picture Show* and had stayed with us in London. He liked her a lot and hoped that we might stick together, for he felt that she was good for me. I think when he heard the news he reasoned that if we had a child together there might be a future for us as a couple, and I might eventually calm down. My dear friend Tobias Moss, who runs a company called Karma Kabs in Notting Hill, and who I met on a regular basis at a cafe called Tom's on Westbourne Grove (and still do!), was sanguine in his approach to my predicament, but he would be for he practised Buddhism.

'Karma is the fruit of the seeds that you sow,' he had said to me.

'What exactly does that mean in English?'

'It means go with the flow. You know, Jason, in life shit happens and maybe, just maybe, this might be the turning point ... go with the flow, Joe.'

Brian Eno, who was my neighbour at the time, told me not to be a 'half-parent'. 'It's all or nothing,' he said.

I was in Bali with my friend Pip when I finally accepted and embraced the fact that I was going to be a father. I'm not sure what made me come round to the idea, but as I stared out to sea one evening I started to feel good about it, really good about it. 'This is it,' I said to myself. 'I'm in.' There was never going to be a right time to be a parent. So I wasn't with Ange any more and our baby hadn't been planned, but that didn't matter. There was no need for me to love that child any less. I wasn't going to be a half-parent to this child. I wanted to play a major role in its life.

On my return to London I called Ange and told her my decision. I would be there for her and the baby, and whether she liked it or not I would support them financially because I wanted the very best for my child. I would rent her a flat, somewhere of her own where she felt safe and secure, and which was within a stone's throw of my place so that I could be near to them both. I would pay for her to have the baby privately and would accompany her to all her scans, and I would be on hand to help her through her pregnancy if she needed me and there at the birth to hold her hand.

I think Ange was rather taken aback by all this, for there was a part of her that believed I would just walk away from it all and not want to know. However, 'I'm not going to do that to my child or to you,' I told her. 'Whether you like it or not I'm here for the duration.'

My daughter, Jemma, was born by caesarean section at the Portland Hospital in London on 28 March 2000, and from the very first moment I set eyes on her I was in love. She was so perfect in every way, so tiny.

'Do you want to hold her?' Ange asked.

'Can I?'

'Of course, she is your daughter after all.'

As I took Jemma in my arms and held her for the first time I was overwhelmed by the emotion of it all and broke into tears, for I realised that I had just been given the most precious gift in my life, and it was all thanks to Ange.

Chapter Twenty-One

Three Good Reasons

As CLICHÉD AS it sounds, it was Ange who gave me my life back, who taught me to live again, who made me see what love really was, and to the day I die I will always be grateful to her for that. Had I not met her, had we not become involved with one another, then who is to say what would have become of me?

I'm not really sure what I think about God, the Universe and all that. Despite my Catholic schooling I have never been particularly religious and I'm not that spiritual either – for when it comes down to it I am pragmatic in my outlook. And yet, that said, I do believe in karma. Life is what you make it, what you give out you get back, and what I also believe – in fact I am now certain of it – is that some people are sent to you for a reason. For me that person was Ange. Without wanting to sound dramatic, had it not been for her I very much doubt I would still be standing. She was my saving grace and set to become the real love of my life.

I am not going to pretend for one moment that there was some great big fairytale ending to my story the night that Jemma came into my world. I didn't turn to Ange and declare my love for her, and I didn't look into the eyes of my firstborn as I held her in my arms and promise there and then that I would never take drugs again. For, as I once said, so wisely it now seems, life isn't a Lloyd Webber musical, and it would take a while for me to finally crawl from under the stone I had chosen to lie beneath for the past ten years of my life. A brighter day was looming, but not quite yet.

From the moment I decided to play a role in my child's life I promised Ange that I would stick to that. I didn't want Jemma to have the kind of childhood that I'd had. I didn't want her to see me on red-letter days only, or to have to meet at some halfway house when I wanted to see my child. If I was to be a parent to her then I would see her at least once a week, and I wanted to be involved in all decisions that concerned her upbringing. I think that while Ange had been rather taken aback by this she was also quite relieved. Like me, Ange had been raised by a single parent, her mother, Margaret, and there had been moments in her childhood when she longed to be part of a nuclear family. We both knew that we couldn't offer our daughter that, but we could make sure that despite living apart we were there for her as a unit, and so for that reason alone we were prepared to put our differences aside.

'Are you sure you mean what you are saying?' she had asked me as I'd made these intentions clear when I got back from Bali. 'I'm happy that you want to be part of our lives, but what I don't want is for you to make promises you can't keep. *I'm* prepared to put up with that, but I won't have you doing that to my child, it simply isn't fair.'

'When I say something, I mean it.'

She had raised an eyebrow and given me one of those looks that only Ange could give, the one that cut me right down to size. She knew I meant well, but come on, I was a cokehead for goodness' sake, and cokeheads aren't the most reliable of people, as she knew only too well from her time with me.

'Yes, but how can I trust you?'

'Because I am giving you my word,' I said simply.

Trust had become something of an issue between Ange and me. When our relationship ended I know that I left her feeling betrayed. I had promised her a lot, but at the end of the day I had failed to follow through. How could she be sure I wasn't going to let her down again?

As it was she had nothing to fear, for as soon as I met and fell in love with Jemma it was all she could do to keep me from the door. I was a regular visitor to her flat in Livingston Lodge, situated on the edge of Paddington. I'd make any excuse to go round, for I was completely besotted with my child. Everything she did filled me with wonderment, whether she was feeding from her bottle, gurgling away in her pram, sleeping in her cot at night, or lying curled up on my chest after her bath. Nothing gave me greater pleasure or pride than when I walked round the neighbourhood with her in her buggy or strapped to my body in her papoose. Who needed BAFTAs and Logies, platinum discs or number-one albums? Jemma was the only trophy I wanted in life.

'Don't you think you should start making your way home now?' Ange would ask after she'd put Jemma down in the evening and I continued to hover over her cot.

'Can't I stay for a little bit longer?'

'Five more minutes and then you're out of here. And Jason ... don't go waking her up again!'

I was still using drugs, still going on the odd bender, but as time went on the lure of drugs was no longer as appealing to me as it had once been. I think there is a moment in every addict's life, whether you drink too much, smoke too much or snort cocaine, when you have to ask yourself whether you should draw a line under your habit. You reach a point where you are tired of the hangovers, the raspy throat, the bleeding nose, the endless cleaning ... up and down the stairs. It becomes boring. I had become like a dog chasing its tale. You realise you want to move on, for it no longer gives you the kick it once did. And that's how I was starting to feel about coke. Although at that stage I wasn't prepared to pack it in for good, I knew that it was doing very little for me, other than to make me feel quite ill.

Now I had a new drug in my life, and that was the love I felt for my child. My feelings for Jemma were so strong that at times they quite overwhelmed me. The night she was born I was on such a natural high that when I got home I didn't even touch the gram of coke that lay on the top of my desk. Instead I stashed it to the back of the drawer. I didn't need it. I didn't want it. I was buzzing as it was, and I got very little sleep for I could not stop thinking about her. When the alarm went off at seven the next morning I was already up, washed and dressed and heading out the door, desperate to see her again.

But as abstemious as I had been that night, I did indulge from time to time, and as I was still using, Ange was adamant that I shouldn't be left alone with Jemma, which was fair enough. So the more I saw of my daughter, the more I saw of her mother, and as time went on we found our footing together again. I sometimes didn't make it home after the late-night feed, and when the sun rose I was on hand to give Jemma her morning bottle.

I'm not sure whether either Ange or I knew what we were doing when we first rekindled our affair. While Ange was happy enough for me to be around, she had made it abundantly clear that we didn't have a future together while I still took cocaine; and if I am honest about it I was reluctant to commit to her. I was terrified of putting myself on the line, only to let her down again, and I just didn't know what I wanted at the time. But as much as we had our reservations and doubts, what was clear to both of us was that the attraction was still there. We simply couldn't let go.

'It's positive,' she said to me one morning.

'Are you sure?'

'I've done the test twice now.'

'Oh my god!'

'Are you angry with me?'

'No, no, not at all. I'm sorry, that came out the wrong way ... I couldn't be happier, I'm thrilled! It's amazing ... I can't believe I am going to be a father all over again! Another little chicken.'

When I called Dad to tell him the news he was thrilled. He'd come to London earlier that year to meet his first grandchild and had completely fallen for her, so he was excited about the prospect of having another one. But there was another reason as to why he was so happy for me, and that was because he thought I finally had a chance of turning my life around for good.

My son, Zac, was born on 23 March 2001, five days before Jemma celebrated her first birthday, making the brother and sister Irish twins. I feel a bit bad about this now, for Ange didn't have the easiest of times during Zac's birth, but as I was still reeling from the bill from the Portland Hospital we cut a few corners when it came to him, and had booked into a local hospital, not that he was any the wiser.

I was both proud and pleased to have a son, not least because everyone kept telling me he was the spitting image of me – although to give him his dues Zac had a little more hair than his old man. 'A girl and a boy,' the nurse said to me when she came to check on Ange that night, 'the perfect little family.' And I suppose on the face of it we were. I couldn't help but feel the family man as I strapped Jemma into the baby seat of my Range Rover as we returned from the hospital that day. There was just one problem with all of this, and that was the fact that Ange and I weren't really together. We might have been spending most of our time together, and sleeping in the same bed when it suited us, but we weren't a couple as such. And the more I thought about it, the more ridiculous it seemed. We got on well, we liked each other, we shared a similar outlook on life, and we had two beautiful kids together for goodness' sake. What the hell was I playing at?

It was at that moment that the scales suddenly started to fall from my eyes, and I realised for the first time in my life what love really was and meant. Love – and by that I mean real, true and lasting love – wasn't about that sudden rush of blood to the head, that moment of giddiness, that weak-at-the-knees feeling: that was lust; that was infatuation. Love was what I was feeling right here and now, an almost primal emotion that ripped me to the core, that feeling whereby I never wanted to be apart from her or my family. So maybe Ange and I hadn't got off to the best of starts, but it was time to put that in the past. This girl, this woman, who I had so callously dismissed in my drug-raddled state, had given me more than anyone could ever ask for in these two wonderful children. How could I not love her for that reason alone?

'Live with me,' I begged her. 'Move in – right back in. I want to be with you, I want to be with the children, I want us to be a family. That's the bottom line. I don't want anything else from life, I just want you and the kids by my side.'

She gave me another of her looks. God, Ange could be tough at times. I was practically on my knees here and she just had to make me sweat it out. She seemed to have this inner strength that I'd never experienced in anyone before.

'I'll come back to you on two conditions,' she said coolly. 'The first one is that we move house. I don't want to live in the mews with you, it has too many bad memories for me and I want to make a clean break if this is going to work. That house has never been a home to me, and I think we need to get out of the area and start afresh.'

'Okay,' I gulped. She certainly knew how to drive a hard bargain. 'And the second condition is?'

I'm not sure why I even bothered to ask, for I knew exactly what was coming next.

'You have to stop taking drugs once and for all. No more excuses and broken promises, no more lies. Parenthood and drugs don't go together. I don't mind you having the odd spliff, but no more coke.'

I turned away from her for a moment, not knowing what to say.

'Jason, it's simple. If you want us in your life then you have to change your life. You have to get clean. I will not have my children, *our* children, exposed to all that. So where do we go from here?'

If I'm honest I didn't want to give up taking coke; and I didn't really want to leave the mews house or the area for that matter, as I loved Notting Hill. But I had no choice. Above all else I wanted to be with Ange and the children. I wanted us to be a family.

'I don't think she is being unreasonable at all,' Dad said when I told him that Ange wanted to move. 'That house is a death-trap for children. Those glass stairs are a nightmare.'

Since becoming a grandfather Dad had changed, for he certainly hadn't taken such things into consideration when I was a child. But I knew he had a point. My mews house was on a split-level, it was open-plan and had a glass staircase running through it. It was the ultimate bachelor pad and as such wasn't exactly childproof. It was time to move.

As the estate agent predicted, it didn't take long to find a tenant for the mews house. Even though we were buying a new house in Chiswick I was determined to keep hold of my place in Notting Hill. The market was on the up and as I hadn't worked in some time it was important for me to make the most of my investments and watch them grow – for who was to say when the telephone would ring again, as Dad would say.

'What do they do for a living?' I asked the estate agent when she called to tell me she'd found someone to rent the house.

'He's a writer.'

'A proper one? I don't want to have some dodgy guy who isn't good for the rent. I want a long-term commitment.'

'I think it would be fair to say that he has money in the bank.'

'Have I heard of him?'

'Does the name Salman Rushdie mean anything to you?'

Shit! I may not be the most literary person in the world but even I had heard of Salman Rushdie, if only for reasons aside from his writing. Since a *fatwa* had been placed on his head following the publication of *The Satanic Verses* he had gone to ground and had been living at a series of undisclosed addresses under police protection, and I was slightly concerned as to how my neighbours would react to this. As it was they couldn't have been more thrilled. 'We'll never be burgled again,' was the general consensus. 'We can leave our windows and doors wide open if we want to.' Twenty-four-hour armed police protection had arrived in the mews.

So, later that month, Ange, Jemma, Zac and I moved to our new house in Chiswick, and Salman and the police took up residency in my former home, thus making it the safest address in Notting Hill, but not before he had made a few adjustments to the place.

'You don't mind if he makes a few little alterations to the house, do you?' asked the agent. 'He says he'll pick up the bill.'

'I can't see what he wants to do, I've just had it redecorated. What's he got in mind?'

'Well, he'd like to put up some bookshelves ...'

That was fine by me.

'And he'll need to get the house bomb-proofed.'

As much as it was an upheaval, and as loath I was to leave the Notting Hill area, moving house was the easy part, whereas stopping the cocaine was slightly more difficult. Friends and family suggested that I might need to go for a stint in rehab, or at the very least get some counselling or go to my local NA meetings, but I knew that I didn't want to or have to take that route. I didn't have to spend half my day in a room full of recovering addicts and therapists to know I had to call time on my drug use once and for all, for I had the greatest incentive right in front of my eyes. If I couldn't come off drugs for Ange, Jemma and Zac, then god only knew what could save me.

You only get so many opportunities in life to turn things around. This was one of them and I was ready to seize it. I knew that it would take a lot of effort, will and strength of character to drop the drugs, but I was determined to do it. As it was I was getting bored of the lifestyle. I had crashed and burned and was ready to turn the page. I needed a get-out clause. It would require a certain amount of reinvention on my part. I'd have to change my address book, move off the scene for a while, but I was prepared to do that. My life was changing, and I was changing. I was no longer searching for cool, chasing the party, the dragon, the next fix. All I wanted in my life now was some security. Okay, I wasn't quite ready for the whole pipe-and-slippers routine – I was still in my early thirties after all, but I knew I was happiest when I was at home with Ange and the kids.

For too long I had been on my knees, and now all I wanted was to stand tall. I can't say that it was easy. There were times when I desperately wanted to use. I missed that kick, that high, that rush of blood to the head, that taste in the back of your mouth, but I wasn't prepared to lose what I had for a couple of grams of coke.

The move to Chiswick was not an easy one for me, and I guess I never really felt comfortable in that house. I think the very fact that I never properly unpacked, hung a picture or bought a stick of furniture must have said it all to Ange. So when I received a call from a production company in Australia asking whether I would like to star in a low-budget telly movie called *Tempe Tip*, which was to be shot in Adelaide, it was a no-brainer for me. As the kids were so young, Ange was happy to make the move, and in any case we both realised that I had to move forward with my career. I hadn't had many offers of work since I had finished on *The Rocky Horror Picture Show*, and the only income I had was from personal appearances and the odd royalty cheque. I'd be invited to clubs and bars round the country and would get up and perform a few crowd-pleasers from my back catalogue, and while I was paid well for my efforts it wasn't making me that happy. I needed to get out there again, not so much for myself but for my family, for that's all that mattered to me now.

The film wasn't that great but we had a good time, and it was fun introducing Ange and my children to Australia for

the first time. While we were there I decided that I wanted
to reinvest in Melbourne so I bought a house in Toorak. I'd
planned to rent it out, but no sooner had I set foot back in
England than a call came through from my agent in
Australia.

'Jason, how would you feel about coming back home
again and auditioning for a part? ABC have a new drama
on the cards. It's called *MDA* and they are looking for one
of their leads.'

'What do you think?' I asked Ange.

'I think that you should go for it.'

'Are you sure? We could be out there for quite a while.'

'Well, it's not as though we have nowhere to live. We
have a home there, you have family there, and I think it
would be good for the kids.'

MDA proved to be a big hit and I stayed in the show for
two series, but when my run came to an end, in 2004, Ange
and I decided to return to the UK again, as we both knew
that was where we wanted to raise the children. Knowing
how miserable I had been in Chiswick, Ange agreed to
move back to Notting Hill. I'd been off drugs for three years
now, and as I had made that sacrifice for her she was willing
to make one for me.

'We'll just have to make it a little more child-friendly,' she
said. 'And maybe redecorate a bit, so that I can put my own
stamp on it.'

'Anything you say! I just want to go home. I want to be
back in Notting Hill.'

I wasn't sure what my next career move would be when I got back to England. There wasn't much on the table and I was loath to go back on the personal-appearances circuit, but even before I'd had the chance to panic an offer came in: a lead role in a West End musical *Chitty Chitty Bang Bang*. It was a guest appearance, a five-week stint, I was told at the time, although it would later be extended into a nine-month run. Was I interested?

Of course I was interested!

'Where's it playing?'

'At the London Palladium.'

I was back.

Chapter Twenty-Two

Cool Is Being Yourself

HAVING SPENT THE best part of my life dancing in and out of the limelight I have often thought that someone should write a handbook to fame. The book, which I would call *Be Careful What You Dream Of*, would serve as a cautionary tale to all those flirting with the notion of stardom, spelling out in no uncertain terms the flipside of life in the public eye. And for those already basking in their fifteen minutes of fame, it would act as a step-by-step survival guide, a self-help book for people coming to terms with their own celebrity.

Had such a book existed when I became famous at the age of seventeen, having skateboarded my way onto *Neighbours*, I doubt very much that it would have put me off my chosen career – but you can bet your bottom dollar that had I known then what I know now, I would have treaded that particular path with a little more care in the years that followed.

Some years ago I had actually begun writing a screenplay with a similar theme. It's a simple tale about a suburban boy from Australia who is given a hard time at school for being a child prodigy. He finds fame and embraces it wholeheartedly, but soon experiences its dark side. Eventually he turns his back on fame and settles for a simple life in the country. It is rather ironically called *James Bondi*.

I made a lot of mistakes along the way and caused a lot of hurt, anguish and despair to those around me, and for that I will always be sorry, but when I look back on my life today, as I near my fortieth birthday, I don't have any regrets. Yes, there are some things that, with the benefit of hindsight, I might have done differently. If I had my time all over again I wouldn't have taken *The Face* to court, for I believe that it ultimately did me more harm than good and resulted in me entering a very dark period in my life, which I struggled to make sense of. And, as fun as it was to start with, I would never have got into cocaine, not just for my sake and my own health and sanity, but for what it did to those around me. But these are mistakes that I made, and not regrets. So I am older, wiser and a little more weathered, but that's all right with me. I am at last happy in myself, feeling good about being me.

I wasted so many years of my life searching for cool, trying to be something I wasn't. I wasn't content with being a successful soap star, I had to be a pop star as well, and when that happened to me I wanted to go one further and become some kind of a credible rock musician. Kurt Cobain or Michael Hutchence I wasn't, and was never going to be, and there are moments when I look back and find it almost laughable that I thought I could be. But neither Kurt Cobain nor Michael Hutchence lived to tell their story, having both met with untimely and tragic deaths. 'Be grateful for what you've got in life,' Marlene once said to me. 'Not unhappy for what you haven't.'

There was a time in my twenties when I didn't want to be Jason Donovan and all that it stood for. I didn't want to be known or seen as the boy-next-door, teen pop-idol, Joseph even, and yet when I look back on my life now I can't help but wonder why the hell not? I was part of one of the most successful Australian soaps of its time, and I was lucky enough to land the lead role in one of the biggest musicals in the history of the West End, reaping huge financial rewards from that alone, and I also happened to be one of the best-selling recording artists of my generation. Some people don't experience any of this in a lifetime, I've had many bites of the cherry. Maybe the music wasn't that 'cool', but, you know, it was of its time and it worked. Why the hell was I complaining? And what does cool really mean anyway? It's a question I still ask myself, even now.

It's only when you realise what you haven't got in life that you start to appreciate what you had, and that's very much what happened in my case. There was a moment there when I had it all, but rather than be thankful for that I took it for granted, assuming that my life would always be that way. It was only when I fell from grace, and the phone stopped ringing and work ran dry, that I started to see just how lucky I had been.

Chitty Chitty Bang Bang was by no means the phenomenon that *Joseph* had been, but it was a success nonetheless, and when my five-week guest-star contract was extended to a nine-month run I knew that slowly I was getting my life back together. It felt good to be given a second chance and to be at the Palladium again – three years previously I would have been grateful for a forty-minute personal-appearance session in a bar in Scunthorpe – and it gave me my confidence back. However, the most important thing it did for me in terms of my career was to let people know that I still had it, that I could get out there and please the crowds and carry a West End show. As a result of the success of the show I went on to land two more theatre roles, starring in Stephen Sondheim's *Sweeney Todd* and taking the lead in the Melbourne Theatre Company's production of *Festen*.

'Where's Jason Donovan now?' the papers would still ask from time to time. Very much alive and working, thank you. So I may not be at the top of my game any more, but there are actually very few people within my profession who can carry on up there for decades, and I would argue that in many ways it becomes more difficult for a man to reinvent himself as he grows older. I am always faintly amused when journalists and reviewers comment on how I have aged in articles – it is almost as though they expect me to walk into a room or onto a stage and still look like I did during my glory days in *Neigh-*

hours. But that was twenty years ago now. Yes, I have aged; yes, I have lost some hair along the way and gained a few lines under the eyes, but hey ho, it's all character-building stuff. That's nature, after all.

'So long as the phone is still ringing then you don't have anything to worry about,' Dad used to say at the time when I had moments of doubt about where my career was going. 'If it stops, then that's when you start panicking.'

When the call came in to appear on *I'm a Celebrity, Get Me Out of Here* I was in two minds about whether to do it. I had always regarded reality shows with a certain amount of disdain, and thought that by appearing on them you might as well be putting your hand up and saying, 'My career is over, it's official.'

My friend Jonathan was of the same view. 'Mate, you cannot be serious? It's career suicide. The final nail in the coffin. So you may not be up there like you used to be, but it's not over yet – you're still in work and you've got your foot in two countries work-wise. Come on, you are a long way off from being a has-been. Don't do it.'

It was true. I was still working and was comfortably off as a result. But my problem was that the majority of work I did was in the theatre, which meant that as far as most people were concerned I had dropped off the face of the planet. When I talked this through with my agent she agreed – she knew I needed to get my face out there again and get back into the 'hearts and minds of the television public'. She had suggested that I might think about a stint

in *Celebrity Big Brother*, as they had been on the telephone wanting to know whether I would be interested,
but I wasn't. Wild horses wouldn't have driven me into
the *Big Brother* house, for I couldn't think of anything
worse than spending two weeks locked up with a group
of celebs in the middle of winter in London, and with
nothing to do all day and night. Other than feeling
slightly claustrophobic there was simply no challenge to
it. My attitude was that if I had two weeks to spare then I
would rather spend that time with my family at our
cottage in the country. But it was then that the offer from
I'm a Celebrity came in.

It was Ange who suggested that I went for it, which
rather surprised me as I thought she would be the last
person in the world who'd want me to do it. Not only did it
mean that I would be away from her and the children for
nearly three weeks, but it involved going to Australia.

'But that's exactly why I think you should do it,' she said.
'You'll be on home territory, you won't look or feel out of
place there; it's your own backyard. There will be physical
challenges for you to do, and in any case you love being in
the bush. If you have to do any of these shows then that's
the one for you.'

And so, in November 2006, I waved Ange, Jemma and
Zac goodbye in London and, armed with my one luxury – a
pillow with a picture of the kids on its case – I headed to
Australia and into the jungle. Though I could have got
involved in a few more physical challenges on the show, if

BETWEEN THE LINES

only to stave off the boredom, I enjoyed my time there. I treated it like a well-paid prison sentence – I kept fit, made things, thought a lot and made some good friends round that campfire, including David Gest and the eventual winner of the show, Matt Willis. I'd always seen the show as more of an experience than a competition, but I was kind of glad when I came third, for I'd achieved exactly what I wanted to achieve. I'd lasted the distance, I'd had a laugh, the public had obviously warmed to me and above all it was an amazing experience. Sleeping under the stars for three weeks was something I'd wanted to do since I was a small child. Amazing.

'If anything I think it's made you more popular,' Ange said to me afterwards. 'It's done you a lot of good.'

'Why do you think that?'

'I think it's given people the chance to see the real you. Because you have been in the public eye for so long, everyone has a preconceived idea of who you are and what you are like before they meet you – now they feel they know you as you. Not some pop star, or some character in a soap. Even I was like that when we were introduced, and it's always so far off the mark.'

Ange was right about that, for when I got back to London I couldn't really believe all the interest in me. Newspapers and magazines wanted to interview me, television and radio shows were making requests. I'd walk down the street and people would call out 'Jungle Jay', my nickname from the show, or stop me for autographs. On one occasion two old dears turned up at the back door of our country house just to say hello, which was very nice of them – the only problem being they gave Ange the shock of her life, especially as she was wearing nothing more than her night-shirt.

It was a strange time for me really. So it wasn't quite the Jasonmania of the early days of my pop career, but it was something. I was beginning to enjoy a bit of a revival. Things were coming together. I'd managed to get back into people's hearts and minds. Suddenly, it was all right to like Jason Donovan again, and doors started to open for me. In the spring of 2007 I went on tour across the UK and Ireland. Okay, it wasn't a stadium tour, but the venues were of a respectable size and it was a sell-out. My fans might have grown up – there were a lot of young mums in the crowd – but that was great too, for it just went to prove that they hadn't turned their backs on me and they still liked my music. Although I included a couple of new songs in my set, I knew what they had come for, and when I broke in to 'Especially for You' and 'Too Many Broken Hearts' they went crazy – well, as crazy as Jason Donovan fans can go.

In addition to this, I also landed a part in a comedy drama series called *Echo Beach*, and the success of the BBC's talent show *Any Dream Will Do*, in which Andrew Lloyd Webber searched for his new Joseph, meant my Canaan Days also had something of a revival. In July 2007, much to my great honour, I was asked to take part in a concert to celebrate the Princess of Wales's life, which her sons William and Harry staged at Wembley Stadium. As part of a medley of music from Andrew Lloyd Webber's hit shows, along with Donny Osmond and Lee Mead (the winner of the search for Joseph), I had to perform a rendition of 'Any Dream Will Do'. I've sung that song so many times in my life, so in the run-up to the concert I wasn't nervous about it, but as I stood in the wings it suddenly struck me that I was going out on stage in front of 70,000 people – 'make that 150 million, mate, if you include all the people watching it on telly' a roadie rather unhelpfully told me just as I was about to go on – but it wasn't those figures that overwhelmed me, it was the fact that I was there at all.

At the after-show party, which was staged at Wembley Arena, for security reasons, like all the other acts who performed that night, I was having difficulty getting my family into the VIP area where princes William and Harry were going to be. I could go in, but Ange and the kids could not, I was told firmly by the security guards. Well, that's all very well and good, but these days I come as a package, and if that was the case then I decided I'd rather go home with them. I wasn't happy! This wasn't helping anyone, especially Jemma, who was crying because it was her dream to meet a real-life prince. We were standing in the corridor and I was about to turn on my heel when I saw William and Harry coming towards me. They came over to congratulate me for my performance, and as they did so I asked William if he wouldn't mind saying hello to Jemma because she was desperate to meet him. I know it was a little cheeky of me as

I am sure they were keen to get into the party, but faced with breaking royal protocol versus my daughter's bedtime tears I thought I'd chance it. William didn't even balk at the idea and went straight over to Jemma, crouched down to her level, just like his mother would have done, and had a chat with her. It can't have lasted more than thirty seconds but since then she has never stopped talking about it.

It's a funny thing, life. One minute your world seems so dark you cannot imagine that you will ever find a path out of that place. If you had told me eight years ago, while I was destroying my body, mind, soul and career with cocaine, that I would one day bounce back, I wouldn't have believed you. And yet, here I am, back on the scene with a career ahead of me again and, among other things, playing for royalty. The phone rings, the offers come in on the table. Despite being older I am healthier than ever, and even though I like to indulge in the odd glass of wine from time to time I haven't touched cocaine from the day I vowed to give it up six years ago. I have two gorgeous kids and Ange, for whom my love just seems to grow and grow. It astounds me. Amazing ... I look at my children as I watch them grow and wonder what I ever did to deserve them – to deserve it all, really.

I was on tour in Ireland recently, staying at a lovely hotel in Dublin, and when I got back from the gig that night, a saying, rather than a chocolate, had been left on my pillow. It was by Albert Schweitzer and it read:

Success is not the key to happiness
Happiness is the key to success
If you love what you are doing, you will be successful.

Wow ... that said it all for me.

Index

287